FOR THE LOVE OF
TRAINS

An Hachette UK Company
www.hachette.co.uk

Summersdale Publishers Ltd
Part of Octopus Publishing Group Limited
Carmelite House
50 Victoria Embankment
LONDON
EC4Y 0DZ
UK

www.summersdale.com

Printed and bound in the Czech Republic

ISBN: 978-1-78685-269-4

Substantial discounts on bulk quantities of Summersdale books are available to corporations, professional associations and other organisations. For details contact general enquiries: telephone: +44 (0) 1243 771107 or email: enquiries@summersdale.com.

FOR THE LOVE OF
TRAINS

A COMPANION

RAY HAMILTON

summersdale

CONTENTS

INTRODUCTION..7

TRACKING THE HISTORY OF THE RAILWAY.........11

THE WORLD'S RAILWAYS....................................66

FAMOUS TRAINS...94

MONUMENTAL STATIONS.................................115

GREAT TRAIN JOURNEYS..................................135

CONQUERING THE LANDSCAPE.......................153

STARS OF SCREEN...170

CAPTURING THE MAGIC....................................184

KEEPING THE DREAM ALIVE.............................208

BACK TO THE FUTURE.......................................225

SELECT BIBLIOGRAPHY.....................................227

ACKNOWLEDGEMENTS......................................231

ABOUT THE AUTHOR...233

INTRODUCTION

The introduction of so powerful an agent as steam to a carriage on wheels will make a great change in the situation of man.

THOMAS JEFFERSON, 1802

This book is an update of the 2015 publication *Trains: A Miscellany*. It takes account of exciting new developments and achievements, including London's new Elizabeth line, the return of the *Flying Scotsman* to the tracks of Britain and parliamentary approval for HS2, the railway that will provide superfast links from London to Birmingham, Manchester and Leeds. Further afield, China has been building the 'Steel Silk Road', a twenty-first-century version of the ancient Silk Road, but on rails. This burgeoning freight network now includes a through service along 7,500 miles of track from Yiwu (near Shanghai) to London.

It is a remarkable fact that some of the most recent developments in the world of rail have centred around the steam train. Not only has the legendary *Flying Scotsman* returned to service, it has been joined by *Tornado*, the first brand new steam locomotive to be built in Britain since 1960. For those of us who're old enough, the heritage trips that such trains provide offer a return to the sights and sounds of our childhood (which, come to think of it, I don't ever remember asking to leave behind in the first place).

Whatever age we are, though, and whatever the trains of our particular age looked like, we all remember the excitement of first seeing trains as children. Many of us were lucky enough to have train sets of our own, whether the wooden ones that have to be pushed around the track or the more sophisticated ones that seemingly travel on metal rails of their own accord, sounding and looking for all the world like the real thing. Trains also crop up frequently in our children's books and TV programmes. Not knowing as a child who Thomas the Tank Engine is compares with not knowing that ice cream exists as a foodstuff. Sooner or later we experience the exhilaration of getting on an actual train, chattering excitedly about everything that can be seen from the window. ('Look, a sheep!')

But then something even more amazing happens. In the years that follow, we discover that the joy and excitement of travelling by train doesn't disappear after we have tired of squealing at the sight of a sheep, cow or tractor. We discover the possibilities of rail travel and the destinations on offer to us. Other towns and cities in our own country suddenly don't seem nearly so far away, and nothing can be more foreign than the first train journey we experience in a different country altogether. The shapes and colours of the trains are different abroad, and the sights, sounds and smells of the journey are ones we have never before experienced. 'This is the life,' we think. And it is.

In my early twenties, I 'did Europe' on a Eurorail pass with a friend. We had planned to take in as many countries as possible in a month but loitered too long on the French Riviera before travelling the length of Italy. We managed only two countries (or four if you include the principalities of Monaco and San Marino), but we absorbed them in a way that would not be possible travelling by any other means. The combination of carefree journey and anticipated destination offered by rail travel has always been hard to beat.

I have been lucky enough since then to travel further afield by rail, including a journey on the overnight sleeper from Jaisalmer in Rajasthan's Thar Desert to New Delhi (when Indian families without two rupees to rub together insisted on sharing their home-cooked pakoras and bhajis); a tiffin lunch on the heritage British-built North Borneo Railway (on which pith-helmeted waiters only ever stopped smiling for the more serious business of having their photographs taken); and a trip from Adelaide to Melbourne on Australia's Great Southern Rail. In Mumbai, I jumped onto local trains for a couple of stops just to experience the colourful sea of saris and happy, smiling faces that could not have contrasted more with those of glum, grey commuters into London if they tried.

I have dipped into the past on a number of other heritage railways, such as the vintage diesel Conway Scenic Railroad in New Hampshire, the Strathspey Steam Railway in the Scottish Highlands and the Golden Arrow Pullman experience of the Bluebell Railway in Sussex. I have ridden the bang-up-to-date present on the Skytrains of Bangkok and Kuala Lumpur, and I have travelled on the Jungfrau Railway through the Eiger mountain in Switzerland to arrive up in the sky itself. The fact is, you have to travel to some pretty remote places to be far from an opportunity to jump on your next train.

Whether you yearn for the romantic age of the steam engine, thrill at the speeds reached by today's superfast trains, dream of travelling on the world's great long-distance rail journeys, or long to take the narrow-gauge 'Toy Train' up to the tea plantations of Darjeeling, this book offers you a whistle-stop tour of all that is fun and interesting about the intriguing story and ongoing excitement of train travel.

So hop on board, sit back and enjoy the ride to discover how heptathlete Jessica Ennis-Hill and swimmer Ellie Simmonds helped build the new Elizabeth line through London, why Manchester United might not exist as a football team had it not been for the advent of the railway, and why 'Soapy' Smith had to be shot dead to allow the White Pass and Yukon Railroad to be built.

TRACKING THE HISTORY OF THE RAILWAY

*The time will come when people will travel
in stages by steam engines, from one city to
another, almost as fast as birds fly, at
15 or 20 miles an hour.*

OLIVER EVANS, 1812

While the genius of British inventors and engineers may have kick-started the Industrial Revolution in the nineteenth century, their American counterparts were not exactly slouching around either. Oliver Evans was one such genius on the other side of 'the pond', and he was spot on when he prophesied that steam-powered engines would one day travel as fast as 20 miles per hour, though he understandably failed to foresee the further advances that would allow people to travel on trains at over 250 miles per hour in the twenty-first century. This chapter looks at the history of the pioneers and events that have brought us to a time when we can gallop across whole countries on trains that levitate at bewildering speed over electromagnetic tracks.

Oliver Evans would have been surprised to see us doing so without so much as holding on to our hats.

PRE-LOCOMOTIVE TIMES

There are records dating back to around 600 BC of wheeled vehicles being pulled by humans and/or animals along rudimentary rails for the purpose of transporting goods or even to haul large boats across land from one body of water to another. It would take another 2,400 years for mankind to figure out how to harness steam to generate locomotion, but in the meantime they devised other methods of transportation, most notably the horse and carriage combination on land and networks of canals to cut through the land altogether.

As industry experimented with and improved upon the rail systems they used to haul goods by hand or horse in the eighteenth century, iron rails replaced wooden ones, and flanges (either on the rails or on the carriage wheels) were introduced to prevent carriages from slipping off their tracks.

By 1775, however, Scottish inventor James Watt had created a steam-powered mechanical engine that could turn a wheel, and the writing was on the wall for horses and barges alike.

By the turn of the nineteenth century, the Industrial Revolution was in full flow and there was a pressing demand for a better and faster way to move manufactured goods around. Britain was soon leading the way with a solution – the railway.

There followed a mad rush to make fortunes from the 'rapid' transportation of people and freight. Locomotive design improved exponentially through the trial and error of different components and wheel arrangements, and tracks were soon being laid like mad around Britain and beyond.

EARLY LOCOMOTIVES

The world's first self-powered railway journey took place after Cornishman Richard Trevithick built the first steam locomotive and used it to haul carriages at Penydarren iron works in Wales at 5 miles per hour in 1804. It proved too heavy to be of practical use, but more successful locomotives soon followed.

Salamanca

In 1812, Englishman Matthew Murray built the steam locomotive *Salamanca* and ran it successfully to haul coal along the narrow-gauge, rack-and-pinion Middleton Railway in West Yorkshire. A large cog wheel on the side of the locomotive engaged the single rack running alongside the two rails and the locomotive was the first to have two cylinders. The railway had been built in 1758 for horse-drawn carriages and is the world's oldest operational heritage railway today.

The locomotive was named to commemorate the Duke of Wellington's victory over the French at the Battle of Salamanca earlier in 1812 and gained yet more fame when it became the first steam locomotive to appear in a painting, which was an 1814 watercolour by George Walker, called *The Collier*.

Puffing Billy

Built by William Hedley in 1813, *Puffing Billy* was the first adhesion steam locomotive, which is to say that it relied on the friction between its steel wheels and the steel rails they ran along. It replaced horses to haul coal wagons to the docks in Northumberland and proved so reliable that it continued in use for a staggering 50 years. The oldest locomotive still in existence, it remains a magnificent sight at the Science Museum in London. Its sister locomotive, *Wylam Dilly*, is the second oldest locomotive in existence and is on display at the National Museum of Scotland in Edinburgh. Although *Puffing Billy*'s top speed of 5 miles per hour seems slow to us today, it wasn't then, and it is thought to have inspired the much-used phrase 'running like Billy-o'.

Locomotion No. 1

Engineered by Englishman George Stephenson and his son Robert, *Locomotion No. 1* was built to transport coal on the Stockton and Darlington Railway in 1825. It used high-pressure steam from a centre-flue boiler and was the first locomotive to use coupling rods to join its (four) driving wheels together.

On its inaugural journey to Stockton, it pulled around 500 passengers, making it the world's first locomotive to transport passengers on a public railway. Most of the passengers travelled in empty coal wagons temporarily fitted with seating; others perched on top of wagons that were full of coal. Tens of thousands of people turned out to see the opening of the railway that day, and the locomotive was driven by George Stephenson himself. When the train arrived in Stockton, a band travelling in two of the empty wagons played 'God Save the King' (the king in question being George IV), coal from the wagons was distributed to the poor and the VIPs on board were treated to a banquet in the town hall. *Locomotion No. 1* remains preserved at the Head of Steam railway museum in Darlington.

Rocket

Robert Stephenson's *Rocket*, which had evolved from *Locomotion No. 1*, won the locomotive trials that were held at Rainhill near Liverpool in 1829 to find the locomotive best suited to operate on the under-construction Liverpool to Manchester Railway. The victorious *Rocket*, which travelled at the hitherto unimaginable speed of 28 miles per hour, became the template for most steam engines for the next 150 years. (See the Famous Trains chapter for more information about this renowned locomotive.)

AN INAUSPICIOUS START

At the gala opening of the Liverpool to Manchester Railway in 1830, William Huskisson, the Member of Parliament for Liverpool, stepped down from his train to go and speak to the then prime minister, the Duke of Wellington, only to fall onto the adjacent track just in time to be run over by Robert Stephenson's *Rocket*. He bled to death from his injuries.

Crampton locomotives

The Crampton locomotives that started to appear in 1846 were built with low-slung boilers to the front and huge driving wheels at the back, achieved by the revolutionary idea of placing the single driving axle behind the firebox. Based on the design of English engineer Thomas Crampton, the low centre of gravity of the locomotives allowed them to travel safely on standard-gauge (as opposed to broad-gauge) tracks and they became capable of speeds up to 75 miles per hour. One of the largest Cramptons ever built, the *Liverpool*, went on show at the Great Exhibition of 1851 and helped win the long-running argument between those who favoured standard-gauge and those who supported broad-gauge railways in Britain, more of which later.

Midland Railway 'Spinners'

The 115 Class, designed by Samuel W. Johnson for Midland Railway passenger services in the 1890s, introduced a more streamlined appearance for locomotives and got their 'Spinners' nickname from the appearance of their two large driving wheels. They looked sleek and elegant in their maroon casings, and for the first time largely hid a locomotive's mechanical workings and underpinnings from passengers. The streamlining also enabled speeds of up to 90 miles per hour.

Having been put into storage during World War One, they were brought back into service to haul coal after the war. The last one was finally withdrawn in 1928 and remains on view today at the National Railway Museum in York.

THE FIRST RAILWAYS

The early history of the railways wasn't just about locomotives, of course. It was every bit as much about laying the tracks for them to run along, which presented fresh challenges to the engineering geniuses of the day, men like George Stephenson and Isambard Kingdom Brunel.

The first regular passenger service in Britain was Stephenson's Liverpool to Manchester Railway in 1830, and long-distance routes soon followed, including London to Birmingham in 1838 and London to Southampton in 1840. By 1841, Brunel's Great Western Railway from London to Bristol had become one of the engineering wonders of the world. In 1851, many of the six million visitors to the Great Exhibition arrived in London by train.

By the 1850s, it was possible to travel direct from London to Scotland and when this became affordable for the masses it led to the 'Race to the North' in 1888, when rival train companies literally raced each other from London to Edinburgh, one speeding up the West Coast Main Line from Euston via Crewe and Carlisle while the other rattled up the East Coast Main Line from King's Cross via York and Newcastle. By 1890, the line was opened all the way to Aberdeen following construction of the Tay and Forth railway bridges.

GREAT RAILWAY ACHIEVEMENTS

Forth Bridge

When the iconic Forth Bridge opened in 1890, it was the longest railway bridge in the world (at 1.5 miles). It was also Britain's first all-steel bridge, but it has always had the appearance of iron, owing to the red oxide paint used to protect it from the Scottish weather. The amount of maintenance required ever since has led to the colloquial expression 'painting the Forth Bridge' as a way of describing a never-ending task.

TAY BRIDGE COLLAPSE

The first railway bridge built over the Tay in 1878 lasted just 19 months before collapsing during a force-10 gale in late December 1879. A train with six carriages carrying 75 passengers and crew was crossing at the time and plunged into the freezing waters below, with no survivors. It was replaced by the second Tay Bridge in 1887, but you can still see the stumps of the original structure poking out of the water below.

Man versus geography

Laying tracks across flat, solid terrain is one thing. Laying tracks across hills, mountains, valleys, rivers and marshland is quite another. Such natural obstacles had to be conquered by means of bridges, viaducts, embankments and tunnels, and it is one of the great legacies of Victorian engineering that most of the solutions devised by those railway pioneers remain intact and fully functioning today. Let's have a closer look at the two greatest pioneers of all.

George Stephenson (1781–1848)

In many ways, George Stephenson was the J. M. W. Turner of the engineering world. As contemporary geniuses born on the wrong side of the tracks, they each had to overcome the ridicule of their respective establishments to make their way in life. Turner fought the art establishment and won. Stephenson, an illiterate self-educated maverick from Newcastle upon Tyne, was initially laughed out of the House of Commons after trying to persuade Members about the merits of his hare-brained railway schemes. After he started to conquer valleys and rivers and peat bogs with his engineering prowess, however, they stopped laughing and started investing.

Stephenson is today heralded as the 'Father of the Railways'. His achievements, as we have seen, included the first steam locomotive service to carry passengers and the world's first intercity railway service, the Liverpool to Manchester Railway. A series of difficult cuttings, embankments and viaducts were required to complete the line from Liverpool to Manchester, but his greatest challenge was how to cross the peat bog of Chat Moss at Salford, which he overcame by effectively floating the line over a foundation of heather, branches and stones.

Stephenson appeared on the reverse of the Bank of England £5 note from 1990 until 2003, alongside an engraving of *Rocket*, which he helped his son Robert to design and build. Perhaps his greatest claim to fame, though, is that he is widely believed to have inspired the Geordie nickname given to all natives of Tyneside to this day, because he was known locally as 'Geordie the engine-wright' and he invented the 'Geordie lamp', a miner's lamp that he produced around the same time as Humphry Davy invented the Davy lamp used elsewhere in the country.

Isambard Kingdom Brunel (1806–1859)

Brunel was appointed chief engineer of the Great Western Railway (GWR) in 1833, at the age of just 27. Within eight years the line from London to Bristol had incorporated numerous engineering firsts, including the Maidenhead Railway Bridge (the flattest and widest brick-arch bridge in the world at that time) and the 2-mile-long Box Tunnel between Bath and Chippenham.

His non-railway achievements were no less impressive, and included the SS *Great Western* paddle-wheel steamship, so called because Brunel envisaged effectively extending the Great Western Railway to New York by allowing passengers to buy a single through ticket from London, with just one change needed from the Great Western Railway to the Great Western Steamship Company at Bristol. He is immortalised in the name of Brunel University, and in 2002 he came second behind Winston Churchill in the BBC poll to establish the '100 Greatest Britons'. In 2006, the Royal Mint struck a £2 coin depicting Brunel and the roof of Paddington Station, which he also designed.

TRAIN OF THOUGHT
FAST-FLOWING RUGBY

If you've ever thought how convenient Cardiff Central Station is for the city's two great rugby stadiums, Cardiff Arms Park and the Millennium Stadium, thank Isambard Kingdom Brunel. The River

Taff once had a bit of a kink right where Brunel wanted to build the station, so he diverted it out of the way (nothing was allowed to get in the way of the Great Western Railway). After the station opened in 1850, the Bute family, who owned the reclaimed land between the station and the new path of the river, decided to give it over to the people of Cardiff for recreation and sport. Voila! (as they say in the Valleys).

George Stephenson and Brunel might be the best-known of the nineteenth-century railway engineers, but others made significant contributions. In 1832, Charles Fox invented the railway switch, or points, which allowed trains to run freely when diverting from one track to another. In 1834, William Dargan built the Dublin and Kingstown Railway, widely believed to have provided the first dedicated commuter service in the world, because its primary purpose was to transport men between their homes in Dublin and their workplace at the docks. And then, of course, there were the navvies, without whom men like Stephenson and Brunel could not have realised their railway dreams at all.

Navvies
In the first 50 years of railway building in Britain alone, millions of navvies dug through enough earth and rock to create a network that was the equivalent of digging to Australia and back. It is no surprise that they earned a reputation as hard men, but they had in fact started off as skilled navigators (hence 'navvies'), as they were often the only people who could figure out the way across difficult terrain when it came right down to it. So they weren't exactly soft in the head either.

The 'gauge wars'

In 1830, George Stephenson had been able to use revolutionary wrought-iron track, which was much stronger than the cast iron previously used, when building the Liverpool to Manchester Railway. By the 1860s, the advent of more durable and comparatively inexpensive steel allowed the transition from wrought iron, resulting in a further boom for the networks being built around the world. This improvement, though, did not address the much thornier issue of how far apart to set the rails, whatever they were made of.

► **Narrow gauge**: these railways were cheaper to build than anything else and better suited to the tight twists and turns of mountainous terrain and industrial areas such as ports. They went on to serve industry worldwide for a hundred years.

► **Standard gauge**: George Stephenson set this at 4 feet 8½ inches on his railways. It was more suited to fast, level track, but not all railway companies fell into line with the Stephenson standard and many developed their own 'standards' instead.

► **Broad gauge**: Brunel used a broader gauge of 7 feet and a ¼ of an inch on the Great Western Railway, believing that it would allow safer travel at high speeds and because it could carry larger, heavier trains, which meant more revenue for the GWR.

The Regulating the Gauge of Railways Act was passed in 1846 in Britain to end the 'gauge wars' and sort out the mess caused by the incompatibility of the different 'standard' gauges being used by railways around the country. It ruled in favour of

Stephenson, but the Great Western Railway remained a law unto itself and did not fully convert to Stephenson's standard gauge until 1892.

Today, over 60 per cent of the world's rail networks, and almost all of its high-speed track, operate on Stephenson's standard gauge. Broader gauges remain prevalent on the Indian subcontinent and throughout Russia and eastern Europe, because they are more suited to the heavier trains used in those parts of the world.

THE FIRST RAILWAY STATIONS

The first railway stations were built at either end of the Liverpool to Manchester Railway in 1830. By 1836, London's first railway station had opened at London Bridge and by the end of the century thirteen London termini were up and running (we will look more closely at King's Cross and St Pancras in the Monumental Stations chapter). Inspired by the Crystal Palace built in Hyde Park for the Great Exhibition three years earlier, Brunel's groundbreaking design for Paddington in 1854 established the cathedral-like structure of glazed roofs supported by tall wrought-iron arches.

The early stations didn't have the plethora of shops and food and drink outlets we enjoy today, but as early as 1848 William Henry Smith had opened the first railway bookstall and newsstand, at London Euston Station. WHSmith stores continue to grace many railway stations to this day.

DIFFERENT TYPES OF RAILWAY

It wasn't just mainline railways that sprang up in the nineteenth century, of course, because the Victorians also cracked on with the London Underground and other kinds of railways were created around the country just to provide fun to the pleasure-seeking masses.

Going underground

The world's first underground railway, the Metropolitan line, was opened in 1863 to get passengers from London Paddington to Farringdon Street (the stop for the Bank of England at the time) and to link the mainline termini at Paddington, Euston and King's Cross. The thinking behind it was that passengers could travel from the mainline stations into the city free of congestion and without having to inhale the smog and pong of manure that permeated the air of the horse-drawn rush hour above. However, as the underground trains consisted of steam locomotives pulling gas-lit wooden carriages, the smoke-filled tunnels passengers travelled in probably weren't that much better for their health. By 1890, though, the City and South London Railway had opened the world's first deep-level electric railway, and passengers breathed a smoke-free sigh of relief as electric trains began to replace steam ones across the underground network.

Just for fun

As the growing mainline network took people to more and more parts of the country, a demand grew for railway-based fun when they got there. Two fine Victorian examples that are still going strong today are Volk's Railway in Brighton and the Snowdon Mountain Railway.

- ▶ **Volk's Railway:** when this narrow-gauge railway was opened by British engineer Magnus Volk along Brighton seafront in 1883, it was the world's first public-service electric railway, and today it remains the oldest operating electric railway in the world.

- ▶ **Snowdon Mountain Railway:** opened in 1896 with steam locomotives, this narrow-gauge, rack-and-pinion railway (think of a train running up and down a zip) took passengers up to enjoy the breathtaking views from the summit of Mount Snowdon. Today it uses both steam and diesel locomotives to climb the mountain.

THE SOCIAL AND CULTURAL IMPACT OF THE EARLY RAILWAYS

We are often told that travel broadens the mind as well as the horizon, but imagine living through a time when millions of people got to see the sea for the first time or got to taste foods and drinks they had never even heard of before the railways started delivering them to their towns and cities. Here are just a few of the momentous changes that took place in the middle of the nineteenth century as a direct result of the railway revolution.

Gravitating towards the big cities

Towns and cities grew like Topsy around this time, as entire rural communities arrived by train in search of work. The arts became accessible to millions of people for the first time, as museums, art galleries and theatres became reachable on a day trip, as did bigger shops and markets.

Even the gene pool changed forever, as people no longer had to spend their lives in the rural area they were born into, and no longer had to procreate with their first cousins just because there was no alternative.

Another unexpected alteration to the gene pool emerged when it was later discovered that many of those who worked on trains around this time used the safe distance between the two ends of the line they worked on to forge new relationships, sometimes even having two separate families on the go in, for example, London and Newcastle.

Oh, I do like to be beside the seaside!
For those who could afford at least the third-class fare on the railways, the world opened up like never before. Holidays at the seaside or in the country, or even abroad, became a reality for millions of people. As well as being exciting, this was also hugely educational if you'd never been further than your feet or horse could carry you. And women became less reliant on men to travel just about anywhere (although, in Victorian Britain, guidebooks still felt the need to advise women to place pins in their mouths to avoid unwanted kisses when going through railway tunnels).

The upper classes benefited every bit as much, because they could now travel further than ever before, and they could also travel much more easily, even with the vast amounts of clothing and equipment and servants that they needed to unwind on a Scottish grouse moor, Mediterranean bathing resort or Alpine ski slope.

All this meant that there was big money to be made in tourism. Trains brought business that would never have otherwise materialised, and those who got rich quick included hoteliers, postcard and souvenir makers and English hop growers (not least because railway workers were paid partially in beer).

The demand for excursions was such that 'monster trains' had to be run to cope with demand. In 1844, one day trip to Hull from Leeds involved 7,800 passengers in 250 carriages hauled by ten locomotives. Fleetwood in Lancashire became the first purpose-built resort to cater for holidaymakers arriving by train, and Morecambe became known as 'Bradford-by-the-Sea'.

Also popular were 'clean-air excursions' to the Lake District, Yorkshire Dales, Peak District, Snowdonia and Scottish Highlands. The poet William Wordsworth campaigned against such excursions to his beloved Lake District, because he felt that the lower classes simply couldn't be trusted to wander lonely as a cloud without trampling the daffodils. He did write a guidebook to the area, which he probably came to regret, because in writing it he had only had the upper classes in mind.

The growth of sport

Sport finally reached the masses. In Britain, football, rugby and cricket leagues grew as teams and supporters travelled by train to away matches; sporting heroes turned up to play in the provinces; and railway stations were built alongside sporting venues like racecourses and golf courses. Even racehorses could now be delivered straight to racecourses around the country, whereas previously horses and jockeys could only race in their local area.

One rather bizarre 'sporting special' that became popular was that which carried passengers to watch illegal bareknuckle prize fights. Two trains would arrive from opposite directions, each carrying their own fighter and his supporters. They would stop beside a field in the countryside on the boundary between two counties to create confusion over which police force had jurisdiction over the area, hold the fight and then get back on their trains to go home again. The government eventually banned the railways from putting on these 'prize fight specials'.

Widespread changes to the British diet

The advent of the railways resulted in many changes to the eating habits of the nation, for a whole host of reasons:

▶ Local delicacies suddenly became regional, national and even global phenomena once they could be transported easily to traders around the country and to seaports. They included foodstuffs as diverse as haggis, Eccles cakes, Pontefract liquorice and Cornish pasties.

- ▶ Exotic foreign foodstuffs arriving at UK ports could also be delivered far and wide around the country. Bananas, for example, could be ripened on the move with steam pumped from the locomotive, ready to eat when they arrived at local markets.

- ▶ The advent of the railways created the modern trawling industry and made fish affordable. For those who had never been to a seaside, the sight and smell of all that fresh fish and seafood would have been a new experience. Without the advent of the railways, fish and chips would never have become a national dish.

- ▶ Many train routes became known by the produce they delivered to London markets for the first time, e.g. the Turkey Line, the Watercress Line.

- ▶ The quantity of food available to Londoners was augmented, and huge profits were made by bringing fresh meat quickly to Smithfield Market from Ireland by ship and then train, but it left many Irish starving as a result.

- ▶ It became possible to go on shopping expeditions to towns and cities by train and get your purchases home the same day.

- ▶ Brand advertising became a thing in view of the choice now available to the consumer and because enamel advertising signs put up in railway stations could be seen by huge numbers of rail passengers.

- ▶ Supermarkets like Sainsbury's were created in the vicinity of railway stations to take advantage of the wide variety of goods now available.

FEAR OF THE UNKNOWN

Change on a grand scale is exciting to many, but to others it brings on a fear of the unknown. In the case of railways, it caused what became known medically as siderodromophobia, from the Greek *sidero* (iron), *dromo* (racecourse) and *phobia* (fear). Here are some of the less rational fears that people felt at the sight of the first iron monsters in the nineteenth century.

- ▶ As it won't be possible to breathe travelling at 30 miles per hour or more, it is bound to result in collapsed lungs and ribcages.

- ▶ The human eye will be damaged by having to adjust to such constant motion.

- ▶ Cows grazing in fields near passing trains will produce stale milk.

- ▶ The smoke will blacken the fleeces of sheep.

- ▶ Poor people from the country will travel on trains to the cities and pick rich people's pockets when they get there.

Queen Victoria herself was wary of the railways at first, so many of her subjects were probably encouraged to see her finally overcome her fear and take what would prove to be the first of her many train journeys in 1842. In fact, the railways allowed her to meet a lot more of her subjects and to more easily visit her favourite residences at Balmoral in the Scottish Highlands and Osborne House on the Isle of Wight.

TRAIN OF THOUGHT
RIP THEIR FLESH OFF!

They took rail-passenger behaviour seriously in nineteenth-century Ireland, with jail sentences handed out for even minor offences. One nine-year-old child was sent to jail for annoying other passengers while playing with some marbles. If that scale of justice were to be applied to present-day rail travel, passengers who scream into mobile phones with their mouths full of half-chewed burger would presumably be sentenced to have their flesh ripped off by rabid dogs. Just saying.

GETTING THE TIMING RIGHT

The more people travelled by train, the more important it became to let them know in advance about departure and arrival times. In 1839, George Bradshaw's publishing company in Manchester produced the first-ever compilation of railway timetables (we will return to George Bradshaw at the start of the Great Train Journeys chapter), but there remained the not inconsiderable issue that the people of Britain did not set their clocks to a uniform time (Bristol, for example, was 14 minutes behind London), which was a throwback to the need for people to work their farms according to the daylight available to them.

In 1840, the Great Western Railway adopted 'London Time' (GMT) across its network to help people avoid missing trains and to reduce the likelihood of accidents caused by the different timetables in use around the country. Following some initial pockets of resistance from towns and cities that felt no need to give up their 'independence' just to kowtow to London, a standard railway time was soon enough being adopted throughout Britain.

It took a bit longer to bring Ireland into line. Around the turn of the twentieth century, Belfast Railway Station, in deference to the political sensitivities prevailing at the time, displayed two different times on the same clock dial: Dublin Mean Time (which was 25 minutes 21 seconds behind GMT) and Belfast Mean Time (which was 23 minutes 39 seconds behind GMT). It follows that passengers had to adjust their watches by 1 minute 42 seconds whenever they crossed the border between north and south, even though there wasn't in fact a border because all of Ireland was a part of the United Kingdom of Great Britain and Ireland at the time.

The arrival of a uniform time and the availability of timetables did have one unfortunate effect – it raised the expectations of railway passengers and gave rise to the British malaise of complaining about even short delays. The age of the grumpy commuter was born.

TRAIN OF THOUGHT
TO PADDINGTON. STOP. PLEASE CATCH MURDERER. STOP.

Railways were responsible for introducing the first information age. Newspapers and mail could be read across the land on the same day they were produced, and international news and mail not much later.

The arrival of telegraph lines alongside railways enabled rapid communication between signal boxes all the way down the line (and greatly improved safety, especially on single-track branch lines). In 1845, they provided an added bonus when a message sent down the line led to the capture of murderer John Torwell, who had fled the scene of his crime by train.

PARLIAMENTARY TRAINS

Lower-class travellers in Britain were originally priced as, and pretty much treated as, freight. They had to stand up in goods wagons that were open to the elements, and even then they could ill afford the fares they were being charged for the privilege. The 'Gladstone Act' of 1844 required that third- and fourth-class carriages should at least be covered so that passengers were not showered in hot coals during the journey, and insisted that railway companies provide at least one train a day that included fares of no more than a penny a mile. Lower-class passengers were also now allowed to carry baggage for free, which allowed many tradesmen to travel about the country looking for work.

The new services became known as 'parliamentary trains' and were run with great reluctance on the part of the railway companies, who often ran the compulsory services only very early in the morning or very late at night. They continued to run 'cattle trucks' for the lower classes at all other times of the day, until the Midland Railway broke ranks in 1875 and started to provide seats and glaze the windows in their third-class carriages. When third class was eventually upgraded across the board, second class was abolished, resulting in the anomaly of only first and third class being available, which did at least have the advantage of maintaining a clear distinction between the classes of the time. Third class later became second class (but not until 1956 on some lines), which later again became standard class, thereby ending the existence of second-class citizens once and for all.

> ### TRAIN OF THOUGHT
> ### WELCOME TO THE WEEKEND
>
> The word 'weekend' first appeared in the Oxford Dictionary in 1870 after towns like Hastings, Ramsgate and Eastbourne on England's south coast had started to offer an early Monday morning service back to London, thereby opening up the possibility for city workers to enjoy a new phenomenon: a 'weekend' at the seaside.

TRAINS OF THE MACABRE

Trains were used for some fairly unsavoury purposes in the nineteenth century, so please look away now if you're a bit squeamish.

I loves a good murder, I does!
In Victorian Britain, people had an insatiable appetite for the macabre, often travelling long distances by train to visit the site of a particularly gruesome murder. When railway companies started to run special excursions so that they could also witness the ensuing public hanging, tickets sold like hot cakes. Executions were often arranged on market days, so that those visiting the town by train would be able to fit in a bit of shopping on the way back from the hanging to the railway station. In the end, the spoilsport government put a stop to 'execution specials' by decreeing that all future executions had to take place inside prisons.

Dead cheap rail travel
The legal and illegal bodysnatching trades received a bit of a boost upon the arrival of the railways, as getting bodies to medical schools and university hospitals was a much quicker

procedure by train, and cadavers were therefore much fresher upon arrival.

At the time, it was perfectly legal to buy dead paupers from alehouses, dead lunatics from asylums, and executed murderers from the state, before loading the day's haul into the 'dead carriage' at the back of the train.

So-called resurrectionists practised a less legal trade, digging up bodies within hours of them being buried. This led to mourning relatives camping out by their loved one's grave until the loved one in question became stale enough to be refused a train ticket on the grounds that they stank too much.

London Necropolis Railway (LNR)

In 1854, the LNR started carrying corpses and mourners between the London Necropolis station at Waterloo and the newly established Brookwood Cemetery 23 miles to the south-west. It was the biggest cemetery in the world and it was meant to ease the pressure on London's cemeteries for a long time to come. The railway was even used to transport lots of exhumed bodies from existing London cemeteries, so that the plots could be used for fresh bodies or perhaps even reclaimed for something a bit cheerier.

There were two stations at Brookwood, one for dead Anglicans and one for dead Nonconformists, and there was further segregation on the trains and in the waiting rooms to prevent mourners and cadavers from different classes coming into contact with one another (you never know what you might catch from a lower-class cadaver, I get that).

The LNR was hoping to get a monopoly on dead Londoners and was all set to welcome 10,000–15,000 of them per annum, but they only got an average of 2,300 each year and no one really got rich on that. After it was bombed during World War Two, a decision was taken just to leave it closed.

INVESTING IN THE EARLY RAILWAYS

In the 1840s, there was a speculative frenzy in railway investment, spurred on by the success of the first railway companies. This proved over-optimistic, and a third of the railways authorised by the government were not even built in spite of the heavy investment they attracted. When the bubble burst on overvalued railway stocks and shares, which were the most important and popular investment on the London Stock Exchange at the time, Charles Darwin and the Brontë sisters were amongst the many investors who lost out. Many members of the burgeoning middle class created by the Industrial Revolution lost all that they had.

THE REST OF THE WORLD SOON CATCHES ON

Other countries cottoned on very quickly to the possibilities and benefits of rail travel in the nineteenth century, and many of them bought British components and engaged British engineers and construction teams to help them build their trains and railways.

In 1830, i.e. later in the very same year that George Stephenson opened the Liverpool to Manchester Railway in England, the pioneering Baltimore and Ohio Railroad carried its first passengers in the USA. Belgium led the way in Continental Europe when it opened a commercial railway from Brussels to Mechelen in 1835, and Germany's first commercial railway opened in Bavaria later that same year, running from Nuremberg to Fürth. In 1851, the line between Moscow and St Petersburg was completed in Tsarist Russia, and in 1852 the British Raj opened its first stretch of railway in India, inaugurating the Great Indian Peninsula Railway with 25 miles of track from Bombay (now Mumbai) to Thana (now Thane) in the state of Maharashtra.

Other developments overseas in the nineteenth century included the following important new technologies:

► In 1872, American inventor George Westinghouse patented the first automatic air brake, which remains the basis of modern-day train-braking systems.

► The first practical electric railway was demonstrated in 1879 by Werner von Siemens in Germany, paving the way for countless metropolitan rail systems around the world – steam locomotives were never suitable for use within built-up cities. The train that ran on Siemens' demonstration line was the first to pick up electricity (from a middle rail) as it went along, as opposed to running on limited battery power.

► In 1883, the Mödling and Hinterbrühl tram system in Austria became the first electric railway to be powered from overhead lines.

TRAIN OF THOUGHT
HOW DOES THIS THING WORK?

Germany's first locomotive, *Der Adler* (*The Eagle*), was delivered in 1835 from the Robert Stephenson locomotive works in Newcastle upon Tyne complete with a driver, because Germany didn't yet have a driver of its own. This was true of many of the early locomotives exported from Britain. If you didn't have any trains, you couldn't learn to drive them!

Prendre le Crampton

The locomotives designed in Britain by Thomas Crampton in 1846 (see above) were an international success, becoming especially popular in France and Germany. More than 260 were built in those two countries, as opposed to just 51 in Britain. They proved so popular in France that the term *prendre le Crampton* remained synonymous with catching an express train long after the locomotives themselves had disappeared from service. One of the original Cramptons built in France has been preserved in the Cité du Train, Europe's largest railway museum, at Mulhouse.

GREAT RAILWAY ACHIEVEMENTS

China and Ireland join forces in Utah

In May 1869, the Golden Spike Ceremony took place in Promontory Summit, Utah, after the huge, predominantly Chinese workforce of the Central Pacific railroad company working from the west had finally met the huge, predominantly Irish workforce of the Union Pacific railroad company coming from the east. Together they had battled tough working conditions and extreme weather conditions for six long years to unite the two coasts of the country they had emigrated to from quite opposite directions. This joining of the continent reduced coast-to-coast travelling times from six months to seven days.

TRAINS AT WAR

It wasn't long before mankind figured out how to make use of trains for military purposes, including in the following nineteenth-century conflicts.

▶ **Crimean War** (1853–56): the 7-mile-long Grand Crimean Central Railway was used to supply British Army troops in Balaklava while they laid siege to Sevastopol during the severe winter of 1854/55.

▶ **American Civil War** (1861–65): this was the first major conflict in which the train played a significant part, as troops and equipment could now be moved to battlefronts with unprecedented speed. In the first significant battle of the war, at the railway junction of Manassas, the South defeated the greater numbers of the North in the Battle of Bull Run simply because they made better use of railways to get their troops into position. Abraham Lincoln realised there and then that he would have to get his act together as far as rail transport was concerned if the North was to win the war. Trains were subsequently used by both sides to carry troops and to supply food and ammunition to battlefield areas and encampments. Locomotives in isolation were used for reconnaissance, for delivering intelligence and even for offensive raids into enemy territory, at which times they usually had machine guns or even heavy artillery mounted on the one or two flatcars they pulled behind.

▶ **Second Boer War** (1899–1902): while the British Army was under siege by the Boers at Ladysmith over the winter of 1899/1900, one saving grace was an early agreement between the sides to allow the casualties of both armies to be taken on one train a day to a neutral hospital, which treated 10,673 wounded over the four-month period of the siege.

ORIENT EXPRESS

Inaugurated in 1883, the Orient Express was the first train service to provide mobile luxury on wheels. The original route ran from Paris to Vienna but that was soon extended to Constantinople (now Istanbul). The decor of the sleeping and dining cars equalled that of the best hotels of the time, and there were even on-board lavatories, electric lights and hairdressing and barber services. The standard of dining was reflected in the following menu, which was served on a test run from Paris to Vienna in 1882:

Oysters
Soup with Italian pasta
Turbot with green sauce
Chicken à la chasseur
Fillet of beef with château potatoes
Chaud-froid of game animals
Chocolate pudding
Buffet of desserts

Those who travelled regularly on the Orient Express included royalty, nobles, diplomats, successful business people and members of the bourgeoisie.

TRAIN OF THOUGHT
GOLD-MEDAL SERVICE

Renowned as the founder of the Compagnie Internationale des Wagons-Lits, the railway company that ran the Orient Express service, Georges Nagelmackers took some time off to represent

Belgium at the 1900 Olympic Games in Paris. He competed in the equestrian mail coach event, which involved racing mail coaches pulled by a four-horse team. As you would expect from the man who provided first-class service in everything he did, he took the gold medal.

MANCHESTER UNITED'S RAILWAY ORIGINS

In 1878, a group of railway engineers and coachbuilders on the outskirts of Manchester asked their employers to help them set up and fund a football team. As the players worked for the Carriage and Wagon department of the Lancashire and Yorkshire Railway (LYR) at its Newton Heath depot, the club that resulted became known as Newton Heath LYR FC. The team enjoyed mixed fortunes in the years that followed, including the ignominy of becoming the first-ever team to be relegated from the top division of English football in 1894. In 1902, they changed their name to Manchester United, but I'm not sure what became of them after that.

A TRAGEDY OF ELEPHANTINE PROPORTIONS

Jumbo the African elephant was the first international superstar from the animal kingdom. Born in East Africa in 1860, he spent time in Germany and France before arriving at London Zoo in 1866 (having been swapped for a rhinoceros that had to trundle off to the Jardin des Plantes in

Paris). Amidst public outcry in Britain, including angry letters to Queen Victoria, Jumbo was sold to Barnum's Circus in America in 1882, where Jumbomania really took off. When he was killed in a tragic railway accident in Canada in 1885 (he was hit by a freight train on a railway line next to the circus), his death was met with grief and sorrow around the world.

INTO THE TWENTIETH CENTURY

By 1900 there were around 22,000 miles of railway track in Britain alone and over a billion passenger journeys were being made each year. The rail companies made even more money from the transport of freight, which in fact provided the bulk of their income. But the twentieth century as a whole would not run smoothly for the railways, with two world wars to contend with and the need to modernise in the face of fierce competition from developing road and air transport systems.

A GOLDEN AGE

Almost all journeys between cities in the developed world took place by train at speeds of up to 90 miles per hour in the early twentieth century. Motor cars and aeroplanes were on the way, but they were not yet ready to provide competition for the railways.

The period is considered by many to be the golden age of the train, and thousands of iconic railway posters extolled the virtues of destinations around the world, from Italy's Amalfi Coast to the Canadian Rockies, from England's Lake District to

India's Taj Mahal. The Great Northern Railway produced the most famous poster of all: the Jolly Fisherman with the 'Skegness Is So Bracing' slogan.

What few people realised during those heady days, however, was that their golden age was very quickly going to be brought to a shuddering halt by World War One.

WORLD WAR ONE

Railways played a hugely important role throughout World War One, with dozens of trains supplying the armies on both sides each and every day. Here are just some of the many ways in which the railways helped secure ultimate victory for Britain and her Allies:

▶ **Sabotage:** widespread sabotage of their own railways by the Belgians greatly hindered Germany's initial invasion plan and gave France and Britain time to mobilise their own troops by train, including the French Foreign Legion troops who were hurriedly brought back from North Africa by the trainload.

▶ **Trainspotting spies:** as most German troop trains had to go through Belgium to reach the front line in France, the British encouraged Belgian citizens to spy on them by posing as trainspotters. Many were caught and executed, but others found ingenious ways of getting the information back to the Allies, such as pole-vaulting over the electric barbed wire put up by the Germans in an attempt to stop them.

▶ **Trench railways:** the Royal Engineers supplied the British Army and its Allies with a substantial infrastructure of railway track, roll-on/roll-off ferries and ports, and railway bridges and tunnels. In order to reach all the way to the trenches, they built a narrow-gauge network, thereby keeping the standard-gauge trains that arrived from England out of enemy artillery range.

▶ **Railway guns:** shells manufactured in Britain in the morning could be fired direct from huge railway guns (usually surplus naval guns) in Belgium or France in the afternoon without ever leaving the track they had left the munitions factory on – the roll-on/roll-off ferries that were used to transport them across the Channel had rails fitted to ensure an uninterrupted journey. The BL 12-inch 'Boche Buster' railway gun fired its first shot in 1918 in the presence of George V and scored a direct hit on the enemy-held Douai railway yards 18 miles away. It became known as 'the King's Shot'.

▶ **Railway workers:** many of the so-called Pals Battalions recruited locally or regionally from within specific communities, trades or sports around Britain included Railway and Tramway Battalions like the 'Newcastle Railway Pals', formed by workers from the North Eastern Railway Company. Such battalions generally went off to fight in the trenches, but many other railway workers with specific skills (including drivers, firemen, guards, signalmen and navvies) were recruited to the military railway companies that built, ran and repaired the railways all the way to the Western Front. Keeping trains running and tracks, bridges and tunnels open was strategically vital to the war effort from start to finish. Back home, 60,000 women carried out the railway jobs left behind by the men who went overseas.

▶ **Supply trains:** just about everything was supplied by train during the war: troops and munitions; tanks, trucks and ambulances; medical staff, equipment and bandages;

food and beer rations; horses and their fodder; and the all-important letters and food parcels from home. Going back in the other direction, the trains were used to get soldiers home on leave; repatriate the dead; evacuate the wounded; and take released prisoners home at the end of the war.

► **Hosting the armistice:** a railway carriage even played host to the end of the conflict, when the armistice of 11 November 1918 was signed in French Commander Ferdinand Foch's former Orient Express railway carriage headquarters at Compiègne in the Ardennes forest north of Paris. Germany was to later hand over around 7,500 locomotives and 2,000 freight trains as part of the peace terms.

TRAIN OF THOUGHT
'THE INVASION ON PLATFORM ONE IS RUNNING AHEAD OF SCHEDULE'

Germany's initial plan in 1914 was to invade France by train through neutral Luxembourg and Belgium. On 1 August 1914, it was decided that the invasion of Luxembourg would be delayed until the following day, but an advance guard of 16 German troops didn't get the telegram until it was too late. They turned up at Troisvierges railway station in Luxembourg, where the locals got to know that World War One was about to start the night before anyone else did. One hour later, the German troops were recalled when the telegram finally arrived, resulting in one of the shortest invasions in history. They invaded again the next morning, this time on schedule, and Luxembourg's railways were soon under the Kaiser's control.

Railway development had been pretty much at a standstill during World War One, but it didn't take long for things to get going again after peace broke out, most notably with the growth of diesel-powered technology.

GOING DIESEL

The world's first diesel-powered locomotive, using an engine designed by the eponymous German engineer and inventor Rudolf Diesel, had been delivered to the Prussian State Railway in Berlin in 1912, and Germany again led the way in the 1920s as the world's train builders got to grips with diesel-powered technology.

Diesel fuelled the transmission system, which in turn powered the wheels, i.e. similar to motor-car technology. Impressive new locomotives could be started with the turn of a key and did not require the carrying of vast quantities of coal and water.

In 1932, the diesel-powered *Fliegender Hamburger* (*Flying Hamburger*) came into service between Hamburg and Berlin, the fastest regular service in the world at the time, with a top speed of 99 miles per hour. A revolutionary pneumatic brake was used to bring it to a halt from its top speed within 800 metres.

The USA was not far behind Germany as far as diesel was concerned. In 1934, the *Burlington (Pioneer) Zephyr* entered service on the Chicago, Burlington and Quincy Railroad in the American Midwest. It was the first of the iconic stainless-steel diesel streamliners that captured the American public's imagination for the next 40 years.

In 1937, General Motors started to mass-produce diesel-electric locomotives for the Union Pacific Railroad. Managing to look simultaneously powerful and Disney-esque (on account of their cartoon-dog faces, which the Americans referred to as 'bulldog-nosed'), they changed the face and sound of rail travel and heralded the ultimate demise of steam.

For the time being, though, Britain stubbornly resisted the trend towards diesel, even to the point of producing the fastest steam locomotive of all time when the famous *Mallard* broke the world speed record in 1938, topping out at 125.88 miles per hour, a record it holds to this day. (See *Mallard* in the Famous Trains chapter for more information about this iconic locomotive.)

GREAT RAILWAY ACHIEVEMENTS

The bogie men

Crucial to the development of diesel and, later, electric locomotives was the need for designers to come up with simpler wheel arrangements than those used on steam locomotives. They came up with bogies that allowed the fixed frame of the locomotive or carriage above to 'swivel' when the train was cornering. The main bogie arrangements designed to carry diesel and electric locomotives are known as Bo-Bo (two four-wheeled bogies, one at either end) and Co-Co (two six-wheeled bogies, one at either end).

THE BLUE TRAIN

The service that ran from Calais to the Côte d'Azur from 1922 became famously known as The Blue Train (*Le Train Bleu*). It was right up there with the Orient Express in terms of luxury, and its early passengers included the Prince of Wales (later King Edward VIII), Charlie Chaplin, Coco Chanel, Somerset Maugham, Winston Churchill and F. Scott Fitzgerald.

PURPOSE-BUILT COMMUTERS

From as early as 1838, communities had started to spring up in Britain for the primary purpose of housing rail commuters who worked in London. Surbiton to the south-west was the first such community and its railway station was even named Kingston-upon-Railway until the community later developed its own identity, and station, as Surbiton. Between 1910 and 1933, the Metropolitan Railway spread to the north-west from Baker Street, creating suburbs that became known as Metro-land, as immortalised in Sir John Betjeman's famous poem of that name. The railway barons bought land as they went and threw up houses to sell to those businesspeople they managed to entice into their new rural paradise, far from the filthy, overcrowded conditions of London. They also sold season tickets on the railway to those who bought their houses, and so the life of the daily commuter became increasingly commonplace.

TRAIN OF THOUGHT
EINSTEIN'S OWN TRAINS OF THOUGHT

Around this time in history, Albert Einstein often used trains in his analogies to explain difficult stuff to less gifted people (in other words, almost everyone but himself). For example, he illustrated his theory of relativity by explaining that a slow train on the horizon was in fact travelling at the same speed as one rushing past you on a station platform, and that passengers seated in a moving train would see a baby crawling along their carriage at a speed of x, while someone looking in from the platform would see the same baby crawling along at a speed of $x + y$. He presumably left it to ordinary folk to figure out why unattended babies were allowed to crawl along moving trains in the first place.

WORLD WAR TWO

Although air transport had come of age by the start of World War Two, railways continued to play a number of significant roles:

▶ **French surrender:** in 1940, Hitler rubbed salt into French wounds at Compiègne by forcing them to surrender in the same former Orient Express carriage in which Germany had been made to sign the armistice in 1918. The carriage had to be brought from a Paris museum for the purpose.

▶ **Large-scale evacuations:** following the evacuation of Dunkirk in 1940, trains whisked away thousands of returning soldiers from ports along the south coast of England. They would otherwise have made a concentrated target for German planes after disembarking on home soil. That same year, over three million people, mostly children, were evacuated by train from the British cities that were bombing targets for the Luftwaffe during the Battle of Britain.

▶ **Taking shelter:** the inhabitants of major cities around Europe took shelter in their underground railway stations during bombing raids, thereby saving countless lives.

▶ **Movement of troops and munitions:** railways became the lifeblood of nations on all sides, not just essential to the transportation of troops, munitions and military vehicles destined for their ports but also to carry the raw materials needed to build ships, aircraft and everything else required for the war effort in the first place. The biggest passenger numbers in US history were reached in the three years following the bombing of Pearl Harbor in December 1941, as troops (and munitions) were carried across the continent to the ports that would transport them to the European and Pacific theatres of war.

▶ **Targeting of railways:** the Luftwaffe caused extensive damage to specific railway targets in London during the Blitz, including Holborn Viaduct and many of the mainline stations.

▶ **The Burma Railway:** also known as the Death Railway, this infamous track was completed under Japanese command in 1943 to supply their Burma campaign from Thailand. They used Asian labour and Allied prisoners of war, who were forced to work under appalling conditions not only to build the railway but also to rebuild Bridge 277 (the bridge over the River Kwai) every time the Allies bombed it.

▶ **Life and death:** Nazi Germany made the most dreadful use of trains imaginable to transport millions to their death, but trains also saved lives, including around 10,000 children (7,500 of them Jewish) evacuated to Britain on the *Kindertransport* (children transport) trains just before the outbreak of war. They were met by foster parents at Liverpool Street Station in London, outside which a bronze memorial was erected in 2006 to commemorate the rescue. This replaced an earlier smaller statue, which has since been moved inside the concourse, and a display in a glass case, the contents of which have since been moved to the Imperial War Museum for preservation purposes.

▶ **Home Guard:** The Home Guard had many volunteers who couldn't join the Regular Army because their daytime jobs were necessary to keep the country running, including large numbers of railway workers, who were often used to mount guard posts at stations and other strategic railway points.

▶ **Women to the rescue:** on both sides of the Atlantic, women once more took on the railway jobs of the men who went off to fight. Their tasks included signalling, welding, mechanical servicing, ticketing and portering. As had also happened following World War One, women generally went back to being housewives once men returned from the war and needed their jobs back.

BATTLE OF BRITAIN CLASS

As chief mechanical engineer of the Southern Railway, Oliver Bulleid built some ground-breaking steam locomotives during and after World War Two. They were amongst the first train designs to use welding in the construction process and to use steel fireboxes, thereby allowing smaller components to be more easily built, joined together and replaced during a period of wartime austerity and a constrained post-war economy. One class of locomotives designed by Bulleid just after the war was named the Battle of Britain Class, in recognition of the RAF's contribution to victory in World War Two, with individual trains named after RAF airfields, squadrons or leaders. The first one off the production line was named the *Winston Churchill*.

In 1965, following the state funeral of Winston Churchill, his body was, appropriately, transported behind the Battle of Britain locomotive *Winston Churchill* from London Waterloo to Hanborough, Oxfordshire, the nearest station to his burial place in the village of Bladon. The hearse van was a spruced-up Southern Railway luggage van and a number of Pullman parlour cars were added to transport and provide refreshments for the great man's family and close friends.

Sooner or later around the world, steam gave way altogether to diesel and electric in the post-war years. The railways of Britain were nationalised and streamlined to fit with the advancing technology, and a proliferation of road building and an exponential increase in air traffic all added to the threats faced by once-dominant railways in Britain and beyond. By 1957, more passengers were travelling by plane than by train for the first time across the USA.

TRAIN ETIQUETTE

As the world returned to a semblance of normality following World War Two, some people found time to consider the more mundane aspects of daily life. Here are two fine examples:

People who find it necessary to vomit whilst in a railway carriage should discreetly use their hats; this would come naturally to anyone properly brought up.

FROM A LETTER TO *PICTURE POST* MAGAZINE, 1952

> *GENTLEMEN, PLEASE ADJUST YOUR*
> *DRESS BEFORE LEAVING*
>
> NOTICE PLACED AT THE EXIT OF BRITISH RAILWAY
> STATION TOILETS IN THE LAST CENTURY (I THINK IT
> MEANT SOMETHING DIFFERENT THEN!)

A FAREWELL TO STEAM

Between 1825 and 1960, around 130,000 steam locomotives were built in Britain at 22 different factories as far apart as Brighton and Inverness. Most were built in Glasgow (25,600), followed by Manchester (20,500) and Leeds (12,100), and many were exported around the globe.

The last one to be built, at Swindon Works in Wiltshire in 1960, was 92220 *Evening Star*, a British Rail Standard Class 9F (but see 'Brand new steam trains' in the Famous Trains chapter for the story behind the twenty-first-century revival of steam locomotives). *Evening Star* was the only locomotive in history to be earmarked for preservation before production even started, and in recognition of this fact it was given a splendid Brunswick green livery and copper-capped chimneys. Having served its time in the 1960s, it was later restored and today it continues to enjoy pride of place at the National Railway Museum in York, playing out the role it was always destined to fulfil: that of an important museum exhibit.

In 1968, British Rail ran the last steam train on its network and banned all railway preservation societies from doing the same, which meant anyone with a steam engine had to take it to a preserved branch line. Within ten years, the last steam locomotive services in the USA had also been retired, although steam held on until the 1980s in poorer countries like India, which could only afford a more gradual process of locomotive replacement.

NATIONALISATION AND MODERNISATION

Having been nationalised in 1948, British Rail announced an ambitious Modernisation Plan in 1955, sounding the death knell for steam and heralding a bright new future of US-style diesel and (eventually) French-style electric. A temporary deterioration in service followed, though, because the initial diesel trains proved less reliable and slower than the steam trains they replaced. In 1963, the infamous Beeching Report was published, in which Dr Richard Beeching, the then chairman of British Rail, announced the decommissioning of many rural branch lines.

TRAIN OF THOUGHT
THE B WORD

Although the railway network in Britain had been built in a fairly random fashion in an age when cars didn't exist, and was probably therefore in need of a certain amount of rationalisation, the name Beeching nonetheless became synonymous with short-sighted politics. This was partly because the cost savings heralded in his 1963 report to Parliament never materialised, and partly because the obsession of the time to switch traffic from rail to road would prove somewhat wrong-headed. Mostly, though, Beeching was vilified by the rural communities affected, who felt deeply resentful at being abandoned by the system.

Beeching was further maligned in the BBC TV sitcom *Oh, Doctor Beeching!*, which ran for two series in 1996–97. It was filmed on the heritage Severn Valley Railway and featured a London, Midland and Scottish (LMS) Ivatt Class 2 steam locomotive and the cast of the long-running 1980s sitcom *Hi-de-Hi!*

In a complete about-turn between 1994 and 1997, Britain's passenger and freight railways were privatised and broken up into a number of smaller operating companies. A separate infrastructure provider (currently Network Rail) was given responsibility for the provision and maintenance of the 20,000 miles of track, 40,000 bridges and tunnels, and 2,500 railway stations.

ANOTHER WORLD RECORD FOR BRITAIN

In 1976, British Rail introduced the InterCity 125 high-speed diesel, so-called because its top operational cruising speed was 125 miles per hour. Its absolute maximum speed of 148 miles per hour has remained a world record for a diesel-powered train since its inception, which means that Britain continues to this day to hold the steam *and* diesel world train speed records.

HIGH-SPEED ELECTRIC

Even while the transfer from steam to diesel was taking place, a new, cleaner and more efficient alternative was sneaking up on the rails – electrical technology that could be used on mainline passenger services. In the 1960s, the Japanese were the first to harness this technology to increase train speeds, followed closely by the French. By 2006, the amount of the world's rail traffic being carried over electrified networks had reached 50 per cent, and now China alone has over 14,000 miles of high-speed network (this accounts for around two-thirds of the world's high-speed rail tracks and is also the world's most-used high-speed network, providing around 1.5 billion rail journeys per annum).

Japanese bullet trains

In 1964, in time for the Tokyo Olympics, the first high-speed electric Shinkansen service, the so-called 'bullet train', started up in Japan, running at up to 170 miles per hour on some stretches between Tokyo and Osaka. The journey overall took 3 hours 10 minutes, as opposed to the 6 hours 30 minutes taken previously by conventional trains. Today, the latest version of the bullet train takes just 2 hours 25 minutes to cover that same distance of 311 miles.

French TGVs

In 1967, the high-speed electric service run by Société nationale des chemins de fer français (SNCF) between Paris and Toulouse, known as *Le Capitole*, became the first train in Europe to be scheduled to run at up to 200 kilometres per hour (124 miles per hour). Fourteen years later, though, it would be eclipsed by the superfast electric TGV.

In 1981, the first TGV (*train à grande vitesse*) ran from Paris to Lyon, setting the 200-kilometres-per-hour standard for conventional high-speed trains that has applied ever since. Before long, TGVs were averaging 280 kilometres per hour (175 miles per hour) on their long-distance journeys. By 1996, they were so successful at getting short-haul airline passengers back onto the rails that SNCF needed to introduce double-decker trains (the TGV Duplex) to cope with demand. They were heralded by the head of the SNCF at the time as 'the trains that saved French railways', and in 2007 a TGV even set the Guinness world speed record (575 kilometres per hour/357 miles per hour) for a conventional train. (See the Famous Trains chapter for more information about the iconic TGV train services.)

GREAT RAILWAY ACHIEVEMENTS

To tilt or not to tilt, that is the question

As the Japanese and the French built dedicated high-speed networks alongside their existing tracks in the 1970s and 1980s, the rest of the world looked on with envy. Those who couldn't afford new dedicated lines, or whose terrain didn't suit, had to come up with an alternative. Tilting trains provided it, because they are able to take corners on existing lines much faster than the slower trains the lines were designed for in the first place. In 1988, the ETR (*ElettroTrenoRapido*) 450, also known as the *Pendolino* (meaning 'little pendulum'), became the first 'active tilting' train in the world to enter into regular service, between Milan and Rome.

Tilting trains are now widely used throughout Europe and Asia. In Britain, tilting trains are used to speed round the many tight curves of the West Coast Main Line from London to Glasgow, but are not so necessary on the much flatter and straighter East Coast Main Line from London to Edinburgh.

CHANNEL TUNNEL

The Channel Tunnel (*le tunnel sous la Manche*) opened in 1994 under the Strait of Dover, connecting continental Europe to the United Kingdom for the first time. At its lowest point, it is 75 metres under the seabed and 115 metres below the level of the sea itself. At 23.5 miles long, it has the longest undersea portion of any rail tunnel in the world (the longest rail tunnel of any description in the world, at 35.5 miles, is the Gotthard Base Tunnel through the Swiss Alps, which opened in 2016).

At first, the speeds attained by the passenger trains run by Eurostar were much faster in France and Belgium than they were in the UK, but subsequent upgrades allowed speeds of up to 186 miles per hour at the UK end of the line as a result of the High Speed 1 (HS1) project, completed in 2007. In 2014, Eurostar unveiled the e320 high-speed train, so called because it can travel at up to 320 kilometres per hour (200 miles per hour). The speed limit inside the tunnel, however, remains at 99 miles per hour.

Eurostar now runs direct passenger services from London to Paris in 2 hours 15 minutes; to Brussels in 1 hour 51 minutes; and to Marseille in 6 hours 27 minutes. After being 'imminent' for years, a direct London to Amsterdam service also commenced in early 2018, with a journey time of 3 hours 41 minutes.

Eurotunnel operates Le Shuttle services for cars and lorries, and their drivers and passengers, from Folkestone to Calais in 35 minutes, and the tunnel also carries international freight trains.

TRAIN OF THOUGHT
QUELLE SURPRISE!

The idea of a Channel Tunnel between England and France took forever to get off the ground (or, should I say, to get under the ground), partly because earlier nineteenth-century attempts failed on technical grounds, and partly because of public opposition and political apathy on the part of the British for most of the twentieth century. It has, therefore, come as something of a surprise to learn that over 80 per cent of passengers using the Eurostar and Le Shuttle services today are British, the people who didn't really want it in the first place.

HIGH SPEED 2 (HS2)

Approval was given in 2017 for Britain's second high-speed rail project, which will provide high-speed services from London to Birmingham by 2026, and to Manchester and Leeds by 2033. The line will be built in a 'Y' configuration, with London at the bottom, Birmingham in the middle, Manchester at the top left and Leeds at the top right. Journey times upon completion of the line will be London to Birmingham in 49 minutes; to Manchester in 1 hour 8 minutes; and to Leeds in 1 hour 28 minutes. According to published government figures, the project should cost up to £46.2 billion and support over 100,000 jobs.

GOING GREEN

Diesel may well remain the primary fuel of choice for trains across vast areas of land (notably North America and Russia) for some time to come, but, as we have seen, the electrification of lines continues apace in many other countries. There have also been some other initiatives to suggest that the future of the railways may one day be greener than it is now.

► **Magnetic levitation:** in 2004, the first commercial high-speed maglev (magnetic levitation) service began in China, with a line that links Shanghai Pudong International Airport to the Shanghai Metro at 268 miles per hour (see 'Shanghai Maglev' in the Famous Trains chapter for more information). This technology allows the movement of vehicles with no moving parts, no contact with the ground, and no need for an electrical pick-up. The resulting lack of friction allows for a faster, smoother ride. The system is entirely computer-controlled because human beings could not react within the timescales of the speeds involved in any event.

Microwave towers take the place of signalling boxes (I promise you I'm not making this up).

A 'superconducting maglev' line is under construction in Japan at the time of writing, between Tokyo and Osaka, which will levitate at 10 centimetres instead of the 1 centimetre achieved by the plain old conducting maglev of the Shanghai line. This will apparently make it safer in the event of an earthquake.

▶ **Urban rail systems:** high speed is only appropriate for long-distance travel, not for urban rail systems, without which the major cities of the world would simply grind to a halt. Over 160 cities around the world now rely on urban systems that operate above or below ground with or without human drivers. These environmentally friendly and fuel-efficient systems are successfully keeping millions of cars off the roads and we will look more closely at some of them in the Conquering the Landscape chapter.

▶ **His Royal Greenness:** many rail companies continue to experiment with running trains on a mixture of biodiesel and regular diesel, but that was never going to be enough for His Royal Highness, the Prince of Wales. Already well known for his sustainable farming methods in Britain, the Prince's 2007 decision to run the Royal Train on biodiesel alone whenever possible proved that he is also a trailblazer in the field of green fuel. In the initial experiment, the Royal Train completed a 900-mile return journey from London to Scarborough on a combination of waste rapeseed and sunflower oil.

▶ **Not such a Mickey Mouse idea:** in 2009, Disneyland California followed the lead of the Prince of Wales with the announcement that it would run all its trains on its own waste vegetable cooking oil.

► **Oiling the cogs**: in recent years, the Mount Washington Cog Railway in New Hampshire has been running many of its locomotives on biodiesel (although you can still opt for one of the steam locomotive runs if nostalgia gets the better of you).

► **Every train under the sun**: in 2014, the redeveloped Blackfriars Station in London became the first to have platforms extending across the River Thames. They are sheltered within the world's largest bridge to be covered entirely with solar panels, which provide 50 per cent of the station's energy requirements.

THE SHEER MAGNETISM OF BIRMINGHAM

You could be forgiven for thinking that Shanghai, Tokyo or Seoul would have been first to inaugurate an urban maglev system, but that honour in fact went to Birmingham, England, in 1984. For 11 years it ran a low-speed maglev shuttle for 600 metres between Birmingham International Airport and Birmingham International railway station, with trains levitating at a height of 15 millimetres. It has since been replaced by a cable-hauled people mover and one of the maglev units is now on display at the National Railway Museum in York.

THE ELIZABETH LINE

The £15 billion Crossrail project that began in 2009 is scheduled to have London's new Elizabeth line fully up and running by the end of 2019, although the first trains started running on the Liverpool Street to Shenfield stretch in May 2017. Here are some facts and figures to give you an idea of the scale of this quite remarkable project:

- ▶ Sixty-two miles of new east–west track have been laid (in both directions) from Reading and Heathrow Airport in the west to Shenfield and Abbey Wood in the east.

- ▶ Twenty-six miles of new tunnels (i.e. twin tunnels running parallel for 13 miles) have been dug under the capital itself.

- ▶ Ten new stations are being added to the network, and 30 existing stations are being upgraded to serve the new line ('upgraded' being a bit of an understatement where whole new concourses and ticket offices have been required).

- ▶ Whitechapel station has needed a total overhaul, the previous station having been cobbled together piecemeal over so many years since the nineteenth century that the underground line there runs above the overgound line.

- ▶ Sixty-six new trains comprising 594 carriages, each with 125,000 component parts and 95 miles of electric cabling, have been built at the Bombardier factory in Derby (on a site that was opened during the railway boom of the 1840s and once produced up to 40 steam trains a week).

- ▶ Up to 24 trains will use the Elizabeth line every hour.

► Each train will carry up to 1,500 passengers; the whole line will carry around 200 million passengers per annum.

► Travel from Heathrow Airport to Bond Street in the centre of London will be reduced to just 27 minutes, and it will take just 39 minutes to reach Canary Wharf on a direct train.

► Eight 150-metre-long tunnel-boring machines were used to excavate four million tonnes of material that is being recycled to create a huge new nature reserve at Wallasea Island in Essex.

► Over 10,000 workers have been involved in the project at 40 different sites, the biggest construction project of its time in Europe. Women have accounted for a third of the workforce, many in key positions such as project managing the delivery of tunnels or stations.

► Archaeologists given access to Crossrail building sites found a Roman road, the skeletons of plague victims, medieval ice skates made from animal bones, a Tudor bowling ball and the bone fragments of bison and woolly mammoths.

► As the new tunnel runs only 17 metres below the concert hall in the Barbican Centre (which is itself underground), the track there has been suspended on springs and sound-proofed with special concrete to avoid the rumble of trains joining in with the sounds of the London or BBC Symphony Orchestra above.

'NIMBY' AND 'NUMBY'

The need to construct railway tracks and stations above and below ground has afforded London's new Elizabeth line the relatively rare distinction of attracting objections from both 'nimby' ('not in my back yard') and 'numby' ('not under my back yard') communities.

GREAT RAILWAY ACHIEVEMENTS

Come on, girls, you can do it!
Following a long-standing tradition within the construction industry, the Crossrail tunnelling machines (which worked in pairs) were named after important female figures, on this occasion with strong connections to London:

▶ Victoria and Elizabeth: queens at the time of the first great railway age and the Crossrail project respectively.

▶ Ada and Phyllis: Ada Lovelace was a London-born countess, the only legitimate child of the poet Lord Byron and an early computer scientist who wrote the first computer program. Phyllis Pearsall was a London-born painter and writer who single-handedly created the London A–Z.

▶ Sophia and Mary: Sophia Kingdom was working in France as an 18-year-old when she was arrested as an English spy during the Reign of Terror. She fully expected to be executed, but instead she was released after the fall of Robespierre the following year, whereupon she returned to England and married Marc Isambard Brunel, who built the first tunnel under the River Thames. Mary Brunel was the wife of Sophia and Marc's son Isambard Kingdom Brunel, who, of course, engineered the Great Western Railway and Paddington Station.

► Jessica and Ellie: Jessica Ennis-Hill was Britain's gold-medal-winning heptathlete at the London 2012 Olympics. Ellie Simmonds won two of her five Paralympic swimming gold medals at the London 2012 Paralympics.

TRAIN OF THOUGHT
WE'VE ALL DONE IT

One thing that hasn't changed much since the inception of the railways is the seemingly endless capacity of passengers to leave things behind on trains. If you told me you'd never left as much as a scarf or a pair of gloves or an umbrella or a mobile phone on a train, I probably wouldn't believe you. During my own commuter years, I left at least six million umbrellas on trains, usually when I'd had a few drinks and always when it was raining cats and dogs as I left the station. Here are some more unusual items that have actually been left on trains, none of them by me:

► Wooden prosthetic arm (probably just the result of a bit of armless fun)

- ► Giant inflatable Mickey Mouse (possibly left by somebody taking the mickey – or not)

- ► Silicone breast implant (bet she was glad to get that off her chest, though)

- ► Wedding dress (not sure if the train was still attached, but it would be quite ironic)

- ► Jar of bull's sperm (not entirely sure how the railway company knew that's what it was)

- ► Two human skulls (now that's what you call a delayed train!)

- ► Vasectomy kit (perhaps it had been left in a cutting)

- ► Kitchen sink (just in case you thought it was everything but!)

INTO THE FUTURE

High-speed levitating trains have grabbed a lot of headlines in the twenty-first century, and environmental awareness is playing an increasingly significant role in the maintenance and expansion of railway networks. Electrification continues to proliferate for those who can afford the infrastructure, and have the right terrain for it, and biodiesel is of increasing interest to those who can't, particularly where long-haul freight is concerned.

Steam, though, has not gone away, primarily because a determined number of people remain committed to preserving what many still refer to as the golden age of the railways.

The future of rail travel certainly looks every bit as exciting as its past, with the opportunities on offer to future generations including everything from iconic steam-driven journeys through the Scottish Highlands to an 8,000-mile journey from London to Beijing with just two changes, in Paris and Moscow. We will look more closely at those opportunities, and many others besides, in the Great Train Journeys chapter.

THE WORLD'S RAILWAYS

We would like to apologise to passengers for the delay of the incoming train from Nagoya. This train will now arrive eleven seconds late.

HEARD ON A PLATFORM AT KYOTO STATION IN JAPAN

One of the great things about the railways of the world is that they are all so very different. Developed independently to meet the needs of their own country's geography, population and culture, they were also subject, of course, to what their governments or industries could afford.

Railway designers and engineers have found various ingenious solutions to the challenges of different terrains, such that railways can travel overground, underground and even above ground. Some track gauges are more suited to one terrain than another, with narrow gauge being ideally suited to climbing mountains, for example, and standard gauge the ideal width for fast passenger services, but neither is much use for hauling mile-long freight trains across an entire continent, which requires a broader gauge to spread the weight across. It follows that the sizes of trains used by railway companies around the world are determined by the configurations of their networks, which means not just track gauge, but also loading gauge (the dimensions of their platforms, tunnels and bridges).

In this chapter, we will look at the current state of some of the many different railways of the world, starting where it all began, in Britain.

> *The train now arriving on platform*
> *one is on fire. Passengers are advised*
> *not to board this train.*
> ANNOUNCED AT BOURNEMOUTH STATION IN DORSET

THE RAILWAYS OF BRITAIN

Today there are nearly 30 passenger networks run by different operating companies in Britain, from the old railway giants like the Great Western Railway to the much newer kids on the block like Virgin Trains. Some companies are regional affairs, e.g. Southeastern Trains, ScotRail, Arriva Trains Wales, whereas others cover the length and/or breadth of the country, e.g. CrossCountry Trains, which runs over the longest network of all and operates the longest direct line, which runs from Aberdeen in Scotland to Penzance in Cornwall. Some are much more specific in their range and purpose, e.g. British Airport Authority's Heathrow Express, or Eurostar's line out to the continent.

Huge freightliner trains carrying goods to and from container docks like those at Felixstowe remain an essential part of industry, increasingly so as British roads become ever more clogged up by cars and lorries alike. The largest rail freight company is now the massive German firm DB Schenker, after it bought out EWS (English, Welsh and Scottish Railways) in 2007. In 2016, it changed its name to DB Cargo UK, presumably to fool future generations into thinking that the country's rail freight operations remain British.

The coming years will see huge investment in high-speed trains and the electrification of lines, and tilting trains will continue to be needed to negotiate the many twists and turns up and down the west of the country.

Diesel will continue to power trains where electrification is not possible or sensible, with increasing use of biodiesel a real possibility to further protect the environment. The new Elizabeth line in London should start to ease congestion across the city from 2019 onwards. In the meantime, commuters to and from the city will continue to suffer on overcrowded trains that often struggle to run on time on a network that was, after all, built for the Victorian age.

Facts and figures:

- ▶ The fastest trains on the British rail network are those used on the Eurostar service to France and Belgium, followed by the appropriately named British Rail Class 395 'Javelin', introduced to cope with the increased demand for high-speed services at the time of the London 2012 Olympics.

- ▶ Around 40 per cent of British track is electrified, due to rise to 50 per cent in the coming years.

- ▶ Seventy per cent of all journeys begin or end in one of London's 13 mainline terminals.

- ▶ London Waterloo has the most platforms of any British station (24) and is the country's busiest station in terms of passenger numbers (around 100 million per annum). It was also the setting for the Kinks' iconic 1967 hit 'Waterloo Sunset', which describes the meeting of a young couple (Terry and Julie, since you ask) at the station.

▶ Clapham Junction, in London, is Europe's busiest rail station in terms of traffic, with trains every 13 seconds during peak hours and every 30 seconds at off-peak times.

▶ Colchester Station in Essex has the longest platform in Britain, at 620 metres.

▶ There are over 150 heritage railways in Britain, an appropriately high number for the home of rail.

▶ Llanfairpwllgwyngyllgogerychwyrndrobwllllantysiliogogogoch on the Isle of Anglesey in North Wales is, not surprisingly, the railway station with the longest name in Britain. Its English translation is 'St Mary's church in the hollow of the white hazel near a rapid whirlpool and the church of St Tysilio of the red cave'.

▶ Northern Ireland, in common with the Irish Republic, runs its trains on 1.6-metre Irish gauge, a broad gauge which can only be found today in Ireland and parts of Brazil and Australia.

BRITAIN'S REMOTEST RAILWAY STATION

The little station of Corrour sits on Rannoch Moor in the Scottish Highlands, and is a stop on the famous West Highland Line that is regularly voted the world's most scenic railway journey. As well as being Britain's remotest railway station,

Corrour is also its highest, at 408 metres above sea level. There is no road access to it, but there is nonetheless a direct service between Corrour and London Euston. If you want to catch the night sleeper to Euston, though, you have to put your hand out to stop the train, because Corrour is one of around 150 request stops at small stations around the British mainland.

The point of its existence, of course, is so that trains can drop off and pick up hill walkers who want to experience the magnificent wildness of the Highlands, far from civilisation and 10 miles from the nearest road by hill track. If you can't manage to walk those 10 miles or don't have the time, just cheat (as I did) by catching a train from Rannoch, which lies 7 miles away to the south. Get off at Corrour 12 minutes later and enjoy a wander round in the middle of nowhere (but be careful not to wander too far if you're not experienced, because the weather can change very quickly there and it gets particularly angry if it finds railway passengers wandering around as if they have any right to be there). One hour later, catch a train going back to Rannoch, where your motor car awaits you on a public road.

Note: There is in fact a very good restaurant on the platform of Corrour station, although it only opens from March to October for obvious reasons. The old signal box has also been converted into three self-contained bedrooms for use in the summer months, which could be handy if you miss the overnight sleeper to Euston because you forgot to put your hand out to stop the train. You'll have to cross the footbridge to the other platform to get your meals at the restaurant, though. If that sort of thing troubles you, what on earth are you doing reading a book about the romance of rail travel?

TRAIN OF THOUGHT
RONALD McDONALD ON THE LINE

In 2002, trains were delayed in south Wales when an 8-metre inflatable Ronald McDonald was reported to be blocking the line ahead. Ronald had flown off the roof of the nearby McDonald's restaurant in Newport after staff had apparently overcompensated for his previous deflated condition.

TRAIN OF THOUGHT
WINDSOR AND (NOT) ETON

There is a station in Berkshire called Windsor and Eton Central, but it most certainly is not. Eton does not have its own railway station because the famous school felt threatened by the arrival of the railways in the nineteenth century and lobbied Parliament to build the 'Eton kink', a giant curve in the track that takes a wide berth around the school to this day. The school's concerns were that their untrustworthy pupils (mostly future prime ministers of Britain plus a few of the world's other despots) were bound to throw stones at passing trains and pick fights with the train-travelling lower classes.

THE RAILWAYS OF FRANCE

The French have been spectacularly good at running railways. From the outset, in 1842, the government decided on a national strategy, thereby largely avoiding the piecemeal and poorly structured networks of many other countries, including Britain. The infrastructure consisted of several major lines radiating out from Paris, plus a cross-country line along the south of the country and a north-south line along the western edge of the Alps. The network was designed to serve as many towns and cities as possible and continues to serve them well to this day. When the time came to rein in the network in the face of competition from road and air in the twentieth century, the French pruned in sensible fashion, even keeping narrow-gauge lines running where there was good reason to do so, such as in the Alps and the Pyrenees and also in Corsica.

Their sensible infrastructure again stood them in good stead when they took the decision to move towards high-speed electrification in the 1970s. As they laid down new purpose-built track alongside their existing network lines, many railways around the world looked on in envy as one TGV after another took to the fast, straight lines. When the time came in 1994 to link up with Britain via *le tunnel sous la Manche*, their trains inevitably ran faster on their own tracks than they could on the slower British tracks on the other side (although, as we have seen, the British side has since speeded up a bit).

Facts and figures:

- ▶ The Gare du Nord in Paris is Europe's busiest station in terms of passenger numbers (around 200 million per annum).

▶ The national railway company (SNCF) runs more than 800 TGV services a day over approximately 1,600 miles of high-speed track.

▶ TGV technology has now been adopted in several European countries and as far afield as South Korea and Taiwan.

▶ The Principality of Monaco is included within the French national rail network.

THE RAILWAYS OF GERMANY

With inventors like Werner von Siemens and Rudolf Diesel at its disposal, it is hardly surprising that Germany led the way with the early development of electrified railways and, later, with diesel locomotives. Nowadays, its growing fleet of ICE (InterCity Express) trains speed across its growing high-speed electric network and beyond into neighbouring European countries.

The current incarnation of Deutsche Bahn came into existence in 1994 as the unified successor to the former state railways of West and East Germany. The largest rail company in Europe, it carries around two billion passengers a year. It also includes DB Schenker, the largest freight operator in Europe, whose operating network spans territory from Portugal to Russia and from Sweden to Turkey (and, as we have seen, also includes the UK).

Facts and figures:

▶ München Hauptbahnhof (Munich Central Station) has the most platforms of any station in Europe, with 32 plus another eight to serve the U-Bahn (underground) and S-Bahn (urban rapid transit).

- An average of around 12,000 glasses of beer are served on Deutsche Bahn trains every day.

- Deutsche Bahn is headquartered in Berlin and until recently sponsored local football team Hertha Berlin, its DB logo proudly displayed for nine years on the players' shirts.

- On 10 November 1989, the day after the Berlin Wall fell, thousands of East Berliners, scarcely able to believe their luck, lined up at Berlin Friedrichstrasse station to take the short train journey into West Berlin.

- Between 2001 and 2010, Deutsche Bahn ran its own television station (Bahn TV), initially for employees and then rolled out to customers. It provided programmes on modern rail travel and technology, and on railway history and nostalgia.

TRAIN OF THOUGHT
A PROPER TRAIN ROBBER

Jesse James and Butch Cassidy found fame and fortune as the most successful train robbers of America's Wild West, but neither of them took to stealing actual trains. That was left to an unidentified train robber in Berlin in 2010. Whoever he was, he turned up at the Deutsches Technikmuseum (German Museum of Technology) claiming to be the owner of two locomotives and a carriage that had been on loan to the museum for a while. Museum staff promptly handed over the keys and the trains were never seen again after the robber simply drove them away. Perhaps the culprit didn't leave any tracks the police could follow?

THE RAILWAYS OF ITALY

Having had no coal deposits to draw on, Italy was delighted when its countryman Alessandro Volta invented the battery and the country later became one of the first to adopt electricity to run its rail network. It continues to make very good use of that mode of power on its high-speed networks today.

Sleek Italian design has also been ideal for streamlining trains. Starting with the groundbreaking Bugatti Autorails of the 1930s (which were actually deployed on French railways), impressive designs have continued with the likes of Fiat's *Pendolino* tilting trains (now used around the world) and state-owned Trenitalia's bang-up-to-date *Frecciarossa* ('red arrow'). The main rival to the *Frecciarossa* today is the impressively sleek AGV 575 (run by the privately owned NGV-Italo company), which offers extra-large windows, wider seats and more elbow room than most trains do anywhere.

Facts and figures:

► Pininfarina is an Italian company that has branched out from car and bicycle design to that of trains, including the interior refurbishment and exterior livery design of an entire Eurostar fleet.

► The train that links Rome Fiumicino airport to the city is the Leonardo da Vinci Express. Try to smile enigmatically as it whisks you towards the Eternal City.

► Completion of the Brenner Base Tunnel (expected sometime around 2025) will reduce journey times through the Eastern Alps from Bolzano in Italy to Innsbruck in Austria from 2 hours to 50 minutes.

TRAIN OF THOUGHT
'SAY WHAT YOU LIKE ABOUT MUSSOLINI, AT LEAST HE GOT ALL THE TRAINS TO RUN ON TIME.'

He didn't really. It was largely a propaganda myth designed to justify the fascist policies of the time. In fact, there were lots of accounts of late-running trains during Mussolini's time in power. What he *was* good at was turning up to take the credit every time a new station, tunnel or bridge opened up on the Italian railway system, but in reality, he was no better at running railways than he was at choosing winning sides.

THE RAILWAYS OF SWITZERLAND

The Swiss got railways right from the start, and a combination of stable government and neutrality in war has left its solid infrastructure intact ever since. With no indigenous fuel supply and much of its terrain in any event unsuited to steam or diesel, electricity was the clear and only solution from the outset.

They built their own locomotives to a simple design that has stood the test of time, but the engineering required to cross gorges and cut through mountains was anything but simple. As pioneers of reinforced concrete, they dug and arched their way through the Alps, with the added joy that their infrastructure was (and is) as elegant as it was functional. Tunnels aside, it goes without saying that the scenery to be viewed from Alpine train journeys is hard to beat.

Facts and figures:

▶ The recently built Gotthard Base Tunnel under the Swiss Alps is the world's longest (35.5 miles) and deepest (2,450 metres) mainline railway tunnel.

▶ The Swiss railways' reputation for punctuality arises from their ability to run their trains like clockwork – like their own precise clockwork, in fact.

▶ The Jungfrau Railway (Jungfraubahn) in the Berner Oberland region runs to the highest railway station in Europe (see 'Jungfrau Railway' in the Great Train Journeys chapter for more information).

▶ Switzerland relies heavily on its rail network on account of its challenging geography and consequently has over 3,000 miles of track, a huge amount for such a small country.

TRAIN OF THOUGHT
GETTING TO THE CORE OF THE MATTER

The numberless Swiss railway clock, with its red second hand in the shape of the signalling disc used by a guard to tell the train driver he can leave a station, was designed in 1944 by Swiss engineer Hans Hilfiker and soon became a (patented) national icon. The Apple company inadvertently used the design on its iOS 6 operating system in 2012 and reportedly had to pay over $20 million to the Swiss Federal Railway to regularise its licensing position.

THE RAILWAYS OF RUSSIA

Not surprisingly for such a vast country, Russia has one of the largest rail networks in the world, even after allowing for the fact that two-fifths of the network was lost when the USSR broke up in 1991. Its mainline runs on 1.52-metre broad gauge, but it also has a lot of narrow-gauge track to serve its port areas and some of its less-hospitable terrain.

Russia is hardly at the forefront of high-speed electric railway development, but it has made a decent start with its *Sapsan* (*Peregrine Falcon*) fast trains on the Moscow–St Petersburg route and other relatively fast locomotives on the Moscow–Nizhny Novgorod (Gorky, as was) line. International fast-train services include the *Allegro* on the St Petersburg–Helsinki line and a through service from Moscow to Berlin.

Russia could only have superfast trains if it changed its broad gauge to standard gauge, which would be a huge financial outlay.

Facts and figures:

- ▶ In March 1917, Nicholas II, the last tsar of Russia, was forced to abdicate on board the royal train at Pskov Station near the present-day border with Estonia.

- ▶ Shortly after the Tsar's abdication in 1917, Vladimir Lenin entered St Petersburg in triumph in the famous 'Sealed Train' that secured his safe passage through war-torn Europe. The train was provided by the Germans, along with gold worth $10 million, in the hope that Lenin could put an end to Russian opposition to Germany on the Eastern Front.

- ▶ All Russian trains run to Moscow time, to avoid the confusion that would otherwise arise from timetables having to span up to five time zones.

- ► Russian gauge (still in use throughout the ex-USSR and in Finland) is the second most common gauge in the world, after standard gauge. It is believed that this broad gauge was initially chosen in 1842 for fear of rail invasions by standard-gauge neighbours.

- ► State-of-the-art double-decker trains with on-board Wi-Fi were introduced on the Moscow–Sochi line in time for the 2014 Winter Olympics.

- ► Russia planned to increase its high-speed network to cope with the additional rail traffic demands of the 2018 FIFA Football World Cup, but it didn't happen (although they did manage to provide over 500 long-distance trains to carry football fans for free between the tournament's host cities).

THE RAILWAYS OF SPAIN

The broad-minded, narrow-minded Spanish took an early decision to adopt a broad gauge, a disastrous mistake for a poor country that could not at the time afford to maintain or expand such a network. In so doing, it also rendered itself incompatible with the rest of Europe, other than its neighbour Portugal (which shared the same gauge). Away from the main lines, it filled the rest of the country with narrow-gauge track more suited to its mountainous terrain, thereby rendering its main lines incompatible with its own rural network.

In the twenty-first century there is only good news, though, as Spain has done more than just catch up with its European neighbours; it has, in fact, created the largest high-speed (standard-gauge!) network on the continent, allowing it to cater for international traffic and to meet the demands of its own growing fleet of impressive AVE (*Alta Velocidad Española*) trains.

Facts and figures:

▶ It is thought that the 1.67-metre Iberian gauge (one of four gauges now in use in Spain) was originally designed to prevent any French invasion by rail, as it would not be possible for the French to switch from their own standard gauge to the broader Iberian gauge when they reached the border.

▶ An almost identical gauge used in Chile and Argentina allows these countries to make use of second-hand Spanish (and Portuguese) rolling stock.

▶ Although AVE stands for *Alta Velocidad Española* (Spanish High Speed) it is also a play on *ave*, the Spanish word for bird.

▶ The Madrid–Barcelona line is one of the fastest long-distance services in the world, covering the 386 miles in just 2 hours 30 minutes.

THE RAILROADS OF THE USA

Ever since the Baltimore and Ohio Railroad carried its first passengers in 1830, the railroads have played a huge part in American history. They helped to tame the Wild West and to physically connect the peoples of this vast landmass, at the same time helping Americans to build a sense of their national identity. Today, government-owned Amtrak is the national passenger rail network, with 30 train routes linking 500 destinations across 46 states, but a whopping 80 per cent of the country's network is given over to freight, most of which is transported by the privately owned Union Pacific and BNSF (Burlington Northern Santa Fe) railroad companies.

Diesel has long been king on the railroads of America, with one impressively muscular locomotive after another hauling its freight or passengers over huge distances. Unsurprisingly, many of these giants found their way into the films of Hollywood, alongside the earlier steam trains of the USA and Europe.

In recognition of the combined need for speed, efficiency and environmental care in the twenty-first century, however, construction is underway on two high-speed electric lines due to open sometime in the 2020s: the California High-Speed Rail designed to cover the 380 miles between Los Angeles and San Francisco in 2 hours 40 minutes (at a top speed of 220 miles per hour); and the Texas Central Railway, which aims to cover the 240 miles between Dallas/Fort Worth and Houston in less than 90 minutes (at speeds of up to 205 miles per hour).

Facts and figures:

▶ The USA has by far the largest rail network in the world, with 155,350 miles of track.

▶ The Union Pacific and BNSF are amongst the largest freight railroad companies in the world. The Union Pacific alone has around 8,500 locomotives across 23 states.

▶ Wyoming and South Dakota are the only two of the 48 contiguous states not served by Amtrak (apparently not enough people want to go there by train to justify the business case).

▶ The Acela Express between Boston and Washington DC is currently the only line in the States with segments of high-speed rail (totalling 28 miles), on which speeds of up to 150 miles per hour can be reached.

► In spite of the fact that the USA has no superfast trains, the US Air Force set a world maglev record in 2016 when they propelled a sled down a track in New Mexico at 633 miles per hour, and Canadian-American inventor Elon Musk's Hyperloop vactrain (vacuum tube train) proposal envisages aluminium pods travelling through frictionless tubes at 760 miles per hour.

TRAIN OF THOUGHT
EAST IS EAST AND WEST IS WEST

The romantic notion of linking the USA and Russia with a rail bridge or tunnel across the 58-mile Bering Strait between Alaska and Siberia has been talked about for over a hundred years. In 2011, the *Daily Mail* in Britain reported that the Russian government had agreed to put up $60 billion of the estimated $100 billion required, but there is no sign of the Americans putting up the rest or having the political will to join landmasses with their old Cold War foes.

THE RAILWAYS OF JAPAN

Somewhat ironically given its modern-day propensity for speed, the Japanese railway system was built on a relatively slow narrow gauge of 1 metre because of its mountainous terrain – although, in 1959, one of its trains did set a narrow-gauge world speed record of 101 miles per hour. It remains largely narrow gauge to this day, except, of course, for its high-speed lines, which required standard gauge from the outset. Since the first Shinkansen (bullet train) ran in 1964, the high-speed network has expanded to over 1,700 miles.

There is a cultural obsession in Japan with trains running on time, including announcements of trains being so many seconds late and, worse still, hour-long delays making newspaper headlines. This national neurosis is even thought to be responsible for accidents caused by drivers determined to make up delays of as little as a minute. It seems certain that this ongoing preoccupation with speed and punctuality will drive the country into the age of magnetic levitation with no end of enthusiasm. Japan already holds the Guinness world train speed record, set in 2015 when one of its prototype maglev trains achieved 374.68 miles per hour.

Facts and figures:

▶ In terms of passenger numbers, the 23 busiest stations in the world are all in Japan (the Gare du Nord in Paris comes next).

▶ The Shinjuku Station complex in Tokyo handles more passengers than any other station in the world, having 36 platforms and more than 200 entrances/exits to control a flow of up to four million passengers a day.

▶ The longest undersea railway tunnel in the world is the Seikan Tunnel linking the two main islands of Japan, Honshu and Hokkaido. It runs for 33.46 miles, of which 14.48 miles are under the seabed of the Tsugaru Strait.

▶ In 1921, the Japanese prime minister, Hara Takashi, was stabbed to death in Tokyo Station by a railway employee who did not share his political views.

▶ The *ekiben* is a pre-packed bento lunchbox that has been sold on Japanese railway stations and trains for over a hundred years. Its place in Japanese culture may be under threat as more and more high-speed train journeys don't last long enough for passengers to require lunch on board!

THE RAILWAYS OF CHINA

Chinese railways had a rather inauspicious start in the nineteenth century when the intransigent ruling mandarins, who felt threatened by encroaching modernity, decided to show the public how dangerous trains could be by throwing bound labourers in front of them. The mandarins responded to the inevitable public outcry by buying up the railways and destroying them.

Long periods of war and revolution ensured that subsequent railway systems continued to stagnate until the latter half of the twentieth century. In 1950, in spite of having nearly four times the population of the USA, China had only 3 per cent as much track. Ensuing Communist regimes then decided that enough was enough, and recent decades have seen a remarkable turnaround. The Chinese leadership harnessed all the engineering prowess it could muster, along with an inexhaustible supply of cheap labour, to achieve unparalleled network growth and unrivalled feats of railway engineering across very difficult terrain.

That momentum has continued into the twenty-first century. China now has the second-largest network in the world (after the USA), and the largest high-speed network on the planet. It is also at the forefront of the futuristic maglev technology, having inaugurated the world's first commercial high-speed service in 2004 to connect Shanghai Airport with the Shanghai Metro system.

Facts and figures:

▶ Rail is the principal method of transport in China, with a total track network of around 80,000 miles.

▶ By 2017, China had 12,500 miles of high-speed network, more than the rest of the world combined.

▶ The world's longest high-speed railway line runs for 1,428 miles between Beijing and Guangzhou.

▶ In 2016, the new high-speed line from Shanghai to Kunming in Yunnan Province (named the 'Shangri-La of the World') reduced the 1,399-mile journey time from 34 hours to 11 hours.

▶ The longest bridge in the world is the Danyang–Kunshan Grand Bridge, which runs for 102.4 miles across the broad expanse of the Yangtze Delta. It was built to accommodate the Beijing–Shanghai high-speed railway.

▶ The highest point of any railway in the world is at Tanggula Pass, 5,072 metres above sea level, being the highest point of the track that runs from Xining in Qinghai Province to Lhasa in Tibet. Personal oxygen supplies are given to passengers to prevent altitude sickness.

▶ Chinese railways follow the pattern of British-style raised platforms and the driving of trains on the left-hand side of dual track (as opposed to the American style of track-level boarding and right-hand drive).

THE STEEL SILK ROAD

Vying with the USA to be the largest trading nation in the world, China is busy recreating the ancient Silk Road, but this time on rails. Its growing freight railway network across Asia and Europe is vast, with destinations as far apart as Tehran, Singapore and Madrid. It also provides a 7,500-mile through route from its huge manufacturing hub at Yiwu (near Shanghai) to London, which is now the longest railway freight route in the world. Passing through Kazakhstan, Russia, Belarus, Poland, Germany, Belgium and France along the way, it takes about eighteen days to travel the length of the Yiwu–London route.

China's task has been made easier by the release of old track that has already been replaced by high-speed passenger networks in Western Europe, but remains perfectly suitable for slower freight trains. For the time being, though, goods have to be transferred onto different trains to carry them through Kazakhstan, Russia and Belarus, whose broad-gauge railways remain incompatible with the standard gauge used in China and Western Europe. The service is nonetheless competitive with air transport (which can cost up to ten times more) and sea transport (which can take over twice as long).

Goods transported along the route include household items, electronic goods, bags, suitcases and clothes (including, one would hope, garments made of silk). Goods transported on the return to China are likely to include British designer items, French wines, German meat products and Russian wood.

Note: There has also been talk of a high-speed passenger network between Beijing and London in future, with a journey time of around two days. I'd be up for that.

THE RAILWAYS OF INDIA

Although rail travel was introduced to India in the mid nineteenth century so that the British could move more freely around the jewel in their imperial crown, Indian Railways had become a very Indian affair long before independence in 1947, thanks to a longstanding policy of local recruitment and management handover.

For many years the company has been one of the world's largest employers (with up to 1.5 million employees), and it carries more than 23 million passengers a day across some 41,000 miles of track to more than 7,000 different stations. Travelling conditions range from first-class, air-conditioned luxury to suburban commuting where personal space is not offered at any price, a problem that has been exacerbated by the relatively recent outlawing of hanging off the side or sitting cross-legged on top of trains. On many lines, live overhead cables had rather taken the fun out of sitting up top in any event.

The British not only bequeathed a legacy of robust, long-distance, broad-gauge railways; they also left behind a number of very different narrow-gauge mountain railways, built in whatever way was necessary to get them up to their respective hill stations to escape the fierce heat of the Indian summer.

These included Shimla (the hot-weather retreat from Delhi), Darjeeling (to escape Calcutta, now Kolkata), Matheran (to escape Bombay, now Mumbai) and Ooty (to escape Madras, now Chennai).

Facts and figures:

- There are no high-speed trains in India, but there is now talk of introducing relatively fast trains on the existing broad-gauge lines.

- Indian gauge is the broadest railway gauge currently in use in the world (except for industrial applications like moving NASA space rockets into position for launch), and it is well suited to the heavy trains required to haul high volumes of passengers and freight.

- Double-decker trains are being introduced around the country in a further attempt to cope with the high demand for passenger services.

- The longest route in India is the weekly *Vivek Express*, which runs between the north-eastern state of Assam and the very southern tip of the country in Tamil Nadu. It takes 82 hours 30 minutes to cover the 2,663 miles, which is an average speed of 32 miles per hour. Not many countries would call that an express.

- The *Lifeline Express* is a hospital-on-wheels that has provided healthcare to rural India since 1991, with one of the carriages set up as an operating room. Painted in all the colours of the rainbow, people can't mistake it for anything else when it turns up in their area.

- The longest railway platform in the world, at 1,366 metres, is at Gorakhpur Station in Uttar Pradesh.

- Meals served on Indian trains are described as either 'vegetarian' or 'non-vegetarian'. Indians have one of the lowest rates of meat consumption in the world, and the train companies have to balance their offerings accordingly.

THE DABBAWALAS OF MUMBAI

Every working day, around 5,000 dabbawalas board trains to deliver up to 200,000 freshly prepared tiffin lunches in stacked silver tins, prepared at home by suburban wives and mothers, to the office workers of Mumbai. They then collect the empty tins and return them to their rightful homes in the afternoon. This simple human system is so efficient that it is held up as a shining example of how to run a business by FedEx, the Harvard Business School and British entrepreneur Richard Branson.

The chances of the wrong lunch being delivered to a worker are so slim that an entire BAFTA-nominated 2013 film, *The Lunchbox*, was devoted to the poignantly comic consequences of just such a mistake – the development of an unlikely love affair. Horrified at the very idea of such an error occurring, the president of the Mumbai Tiffin Box Suppliers' Association described it as a 'masala movie', a spiced-up Bollywood invention. I describe it as a film you should definitely watch.

THE RAILWAYS OF CENTRAL AND SOUTH AMERICA

Neither Central nor South America has anything like an integrated railway network, but they do nonetheless have some outstanding lines dotted around the continent. Four of the six highest railways in the world, for example, are situated within South America: Peru has the *Tren de Sierra* from Lima to Huancayo and the *Andean Explorer* from Cusco to Puno on Lake Titicaca; Bolivia has the Rio Mulatos–Potosí line; and the *Tren a las Nubes* (*Cloud Train*) runs across the Andes and the Atacama Desert to connect Salta in Argentina with Antofagasta on the coast of Chile. Peru, of course, also has the 54-mile rail journey to the destination on everybody's bucket list: Machu Picchu (more of which in the Great Train Journeys chapter).

Facts and figures:

▶ The line from Lima to Huancayo in Peru had the highest stretch of railway in the world until this distinction was usurped by the Qinghai–Tibet Railway in 2006.

▶ The Southern Fuegian Railway in Tierra del Fuego, Argentina, is the southernmost operating railway in the world. Steam and diesel engines transport passengers along the narrow-gauge track to 'End of the World Station', 5 miles west of Ushuaia.

▶ The oldest and shortest transcontinental railway in the world is the Panama Canal Railroad. Running alongside the more famous canal, it takes just an hour to travel the 48 miles from Colón on the Atlantic to Panama City on the Pacific.

▶ There is much talk of the Chinese building a 3,300-mile transcontinental railway from the Atlantic coast of Brazil to the Pacific coast of Peru. If it goes ahead, environmentalists will want to look very closely at the impact on what's left of the rainforest.

THE RAILWAYS OF AFRICA

Although the railways of Africa are likely to remain disjointed for many years to come, the continent does nonetheless offer some of the most spectacular railway journeys on Planet Earth. Most people have heard of the luxury Blue Train and the Rovos Rail Pride of Africa services that have crossed Southern Africa in style for decades, and these continue to excite today (see the Great Train Journeys chapter for more information).

In more recent times, the Shongololo Express service (*shongololo* is Zulu for 'millipede') has added new luxury routes across a number of Southern African countries, taking in some combination or other of Mozambique, Zimbabwe, Swaziland, Namibia and South Africa (with one route also extending into Tanzania in East Africa). Their optional Peace Train service offers the same luxury travel, but with a twist that allows passengers to spend 40 per cent of their time on voluntary projects designed to alleviate poverty and improve health, education and farming opportunities.

At the other end of the financial scale, a multitude of local and regional services around Africa offer the chance to experience very different rail journeys, whether your preferred travelling habitat is desert or rainforest, mountain or savannah.

The first foray into high-speed rail travel on the continent will come with an extensive TGV network currently under construction in Morocco, which will initially run between Tangier and Casablanca before extending to a total network length of around 900 miles.

Facts and figures:

- ► Getting freight, and in particular oil and minerals, to African ports is of much greater importance to local and national economies than providing commuter or tourist routes. By way of example, the Rift Valley Railway of Kenya and Uganda is made up of 95 per cent freight and 5 per cent passenger traffic.

- ► Cecil Rhodes, the British colonialist who made a fortune from diamond mining in the nineteenth century, wanted to spend much of that fortune on the building of a Cape to Cairo railway. The project was beset with geographical and political problems from the outset and, for much the same reasons, his dream remains unrealised to this day.

- ► In Tunisia, the *Lézard Rouge* ('red lizard') train is a unique way to see dry gorges occasionally dotted with lush greenery from a carriage that was previously used by the Bey of Tunisia to get to his summer palace.

- ► The easiest way to get around Morocco's royal cities, and to cross the High Atlas mountains, is to take the train between Marrakech and Fes and stop off at Rabat and Meknes en route.

- ► One of the best ways to see the Nile Valley (and, of course, its antiquities) is to travel along it by train. The line runs south from Alexandria to Cairo and then down to Luxor and Aswan.

TRAIN OF THOUGHT
TRAINING TO BE A LAWYER

While working as a young lawyer in South Africa, Mohandas (later Mahatma) Gandhi was thrown off a first-class train carriage for being the wrong colour. It was one of the events that led him to adopt the stance of non-violent civil disobedience that was to inspire civil rights movements around the world and lead India to independence from Britain.

FAMOUS TRAINS

I could have developed a new train, had I stayed in the railways. It would have looked like the AK-47 though.

MIKHAIL KALASHNIKOV

Some great trains are generic, like the French TGV, and some are specific, like the great named locomotives of the steam age. Great trains are also great for different reasons, whether it be raw power, high speed, sheer luxury or pure romance. Some have been enshrined in literature and the arts; some have even made it onto the big screen. Others became such celebrities during their working lives that people travelled far and wide just to see them.

I haven't been constrained by any particular definition of greatness in this chapter, but I have been constrained by space, because there are so many great trains and we each have our personal favourites. I apologise in advance if yours does not get a mention.

Let's begin, though, with a few words of technical explanation on the early locomotives.

LOCOMOTIVE NAMING AND NUMBERING

Different steam locomotives had different wheel arrangements, such that a 4-6-2 had four leading wheels, six driving wheels (coupled together) to power the train forward, and two trailing wheels. The driving wheels were very often huge in comparison to the other wheels.

In 1900, a Dutch-American engineer, Frederick Methven Whyte, decided to give names to these different wheel arrangements: a 4-6-2 became known as a Pacific, a 4-4-2 became an Atlantic, and so on. Although there are many exceptions to the general rules, you can be pretty sure that a 2-8-4 (Berkshire) locomotive wasn't used on the tight twists and turns of a narrow-gauge mountain railway, and you can be just as sure that a 0-6-0 (Six-Coupled) locomotive – think Thomas the Tank Engine – was never used in an attempt to break the world speed record.

Individual railway companies, having chosen the wheel arrangement that best suited their needs, then set about designing the mechanics and the look and feel of their own versions, or 'classes', of such locomotives. All trains of the same class would be built to a common design, a design that was often so unique that they could be instantly recognised and celebrated by people up and down the country, especially, of course, by ardent trainspotters.

Each locomotive built within a class then had a number to distinguish it from the others built within that class, and many were given individual names as a final personal touch. By way of example, the first 4-6-2 Pacifics designed by Nigel Gresley for the London and North Eastern Railway in the 1920s were designated A1 Class, the most famous locomotive of which was numbered 4472 (later changed to 60103) and named *Flying Scotsman*.

ROCKET

Designer:	Robert Stephenson
Built:	Newcastle upon Tyne, Tyne and Wear; 1829
Railway:	Liverpool and Manchester Railway
Power:	Steam
Wheel arrangement:	0-2-2 Northumbrian
Maximum speed:	28 miles per hour
Main service life:	Liverpool to Manchester
Current whereabouts:	London Science Museum

This is the train that the majority of historians consider the most important of all. When Robert Stephenson's *Rocket* won the Rainhill locomotive trials as a prototype in 1829, it provided the template for the eight other locomotives due to be employed on the Liverpool and Manchester Railway from the following year onwards. *Rocket* itself operated on the line, having been upgraded from its prototype status, before switching in its dotage to Lord Carlisle's Railway, a branch line in Brampton, Cumberland (now Cumbria).

It was a distinctive-looking piece of engineering on account of its tall smokestack chimney and its single pair of large front driving wheels with two smaller trailing wheels behind. More importantly, the family of locomotives it spawned was impressively fast and reliable for the time.

The original *Rocket*, although much modified in the years following the Rainhill trials, can still be seen in all its finery at the Science Museum in London, while replicas exist at the National Railway Museum in York and, across the Atlantic, at the Henry Ford Museum of American Innovation in Dearborn, Michigan and the Museum of Science and Industry in Chicago, Illinois. Buster Keaton also had a functioning replica built for his 1923 comedy film *Our Hospitality*, but its subsequent whereabouts are unknown.

Rocket really made it to the top of the celebrity tree when it appeared in animated form on TV in 2013 as Stephen (see what they did there?) in 'The Afternoon Tea Express' episode of *Thomas the Tank Engine and Friends*.

KERR, STUART TANK ENGINES

Designer:	Kerr, Stuart & Company
Built:	Stoke-on-Trent, Staffordshire; *c.*1890–1920
Railway:	Worldwide
Power:	Steam
Wheel arrangement:	From 0-4-0 up to 0-6-2
Main service life:	Worldwide
Current whereabouts:	Worldwide

Although Kerr, Stuart & Company did produce some larger locomotives for standard-gauge mainline service, what they really excelled at was building tough little narrow-gauge tank engines that went where other engines could not go, and did the jobs that other engines could not handle. They were, if you like, the tugboats of the railway world.

Tank engines were so called because they carried their own water tanks (and fuel bunkers), as opposed to having the huge tenders that bigger locomotives trailed behind to slake their thirst and feed their hungry fires over long distances. Kerr, Stuart made two types of tank engine: saddle-tank (so called because the water tank straddled the boiler) and side-tank (so called because the water tank ran along the side of the boiler). These hardy engines proved so strong and reliable that they were soon in huge demand. In addition to the industrial and passenger-carrying work they carried out all over Britain, here is a short sample of where else in the world these peripatetic little engines went to punch well above their weight:

► Namibia: loading and unloading of ships at the docks in Walvis Bay.

► Falkland Islands: supply of coal to the generators of the Admiralty's wireless station.

► Egypt: construction of the Nile Delta Barrage to improve irrigation.

► South Africa: provision of supplies to siege areas during the Second Boer War.

► Burma (now Myanmar): transportation of mined silver and lead ore.

► Antigua: relay of sugar cane from plantations to mills.

► New Zealand: heavy-duty work at a chemical fertiliser plant.

Many of the engines are being or have been restored at museums and heritage railways around the world. Perhaps the most impressive of these is *Joan*, the 0-6-2T (side-tank engine) rescued from a disused sugar plantation in Antigua in 1971 and now back in working order on the Welshpool and Llanfair Light Railway in Wales.

FLYING SCOTSMAN

Designer:	Nigel Gresley
Built:	Doncaster, South Yorkshire; 1923
Railway:	LNER (London North Eastern Railway)
Power:	Steam
Class:	A1 (upgraded to A3 in 1947)

Wheel arrangement:	4-6-2 Pacific (plus 8-wheel tender)
Number:	60103 (originally 1472, then 4472 from 1924 to 1946)
Maximum speed:	100 miles per hour
Main service life:	London to Edinburgh
Current whereabouts:	National Railway Museum, York

Flying Scotsman was employed to pull long-distance express trains, including the 10 a.m. London to Edinburgh Flying Scotsman service, after which it was named. It was the first steam locomotive to break the 100-miles-per-hour barrier, and holds the world record for the longest non-stop run by a steam locomotive (422 miles).

The locomotive's celebrity appearances started as early as 1924, when it appeared at the British Empire Exhibition at Wembley, and it has featured strongly in popular culture ever since:

- ▶ 1929: starred in its own film, *The Flying Scotsman*, a thriller that included dangerous stunts. At one point, actress Pauline Johnson walks along the narrow outside ledge of the speeding train to get from the carriages to the locomotive – in high heels!

- ▶ 1968: made a guest appearance in literary form as Gordon's brother in *Enterprising Engines*, the twenty-third book in the Reverend W. Awdry's The Railway Series.

- ▶ 1986: appeared in a TV advert for British Rail, who clearly felt no shame about their earlier attempt to sell it for scrap in 1963.

- ▶ 2001: entered the twenty-first century as one of the locomotives in the *Microsoft Train Simulator* game.

▶ 2012: featured on one of the commemorative £5 coins minted for the London Olympics.

Having retired from normal service in 1963 after an active life of two million miles, it has since been brought back from the brink of the scrapheap on four separate occasions (see next entry).

THE LEGEND IS BACK! AGAIN!

In 1963, *Flying Scotsman* was rescued and restored by businessman Alan Pegler, thereby preventing British Rail from scrapping it for £3,000. There followed a lengthy North American tour to promote British exports (1969–73). During this time, in order to meet US Railroad regulations, *Flying Scotsman* was fitted with an eye-catching cowcatcher – the device mounted at the front to deflect cows and other obstacles on the track that might otherwise derail a train (if you've ever seen a train in a Western, you've seen a cowcatcher).

The locomotive then got stranded in San Francisco after the British government withdrew funding for the tour. On this occasion, construction magnate Sir William McAlpine came forward to save the train, paying for it to be shipped home in 1973 via the Panama Canal and for it to be restored upon its return.

In 1988, it set off on a grand tour of Australia (only the Rolling Stones have had more farewell tours than *Flying Scotsman*), following which it returned to run excursions in Britain. In 1996, the

---

locomotive was once more feeling its age and this time entrepreneur Tony Marchington stepped up to the footplate and shovelled in £1 million for its third restoration, but the effort bankrupted him by 2003.

Under threat once more, the train was finally saved for the nation on a permanent basis when the National Railway Museum bought it at auction in 2004 for £2.3 million, which included £70,000 raised by *The Yorkshire Post* newspaper and £350,000 from 6,500 individuals, which was then matched pound for pound by entrepreneur Richard Branson (the rest of the money came from the National Heritage Memorial Fund).

A complete overhaul followed over a ten-year period between 2006 and 2016, after which *Flying Scotsman* finally returned to the tracks, where it belongs. It is scarcely believable that something of that size and engineering complexity could be stripped back to its individual components and put back together again in a way that allows it to run mainline rail tours in the twenty-first century, but that is exactly what has happened. It may have had a few replacement parts, including its eighteenth new boiler since entering service in 1923, but most of it remains the original build, including the wheels and side-rods. What is most certainly original is its soul. It is one thing to be an icon of British engineering, up there with RMS *Queen Mary* and Concorde – it is quite another to be a living legend.

For the princely sum of £4,920, you can now spend five days on board as she pulls you around the Scottish Highlands (there are other excursions to choose from as well). If that sounds a bit pricey to you, bear in mind that there are over 50 malt whiskies to choose from at the bar. You get what you pay for in life.

MALLARD

Designer:	Nigel Gresley
Built:	Doncaster, South Yorkshire; 1938
Railway:	LNER (London and North Eastern Railway)
Power:	Steam
Class:	A4
Wheel arrangement:	4-6-2 Pacific (plus 8-wheel tender)
Number:	4468
Maximum speed:	126 miles per hour
Main service life:	Britain, East Coast Main Line
Current whereabouts:	National Railway Museum, York

Mallard was number 28 of 35 Class A4 Pacifics built between 1935 and 1938. Designer Nigel Gresley was a keen birdwatcher and named most of the locomotives after birds. He made four exceptions at the outset, though, naming the first four locomotives *Silver Link*, *Quicksilver*, *Silver King* and *Silver Fox*, just to keep George V happy in his silver jubilee year (1935). You might argue that a mallard was one of the less exciting birds to be used in the naming process (others included golden eagle, falcon and peregrine), but this duck proved to be anything but lame when it came to performance.

Its Bugatti-style streamlined shape was developed in wind-tunnel tests and lowered wind resistance and drew smoke away from the cab. It broke the world speed record for a steam locomotive on 3 July 1938, heading south at 125.88 miles per hour near Grantham in Lincolnshire, a record it holds to this day. It also looked magnificent in its spruced-up post-war livery of garter blue with red and white lining.

It served its time on the East Coast Main Line, gracing the Yorkshire Pullman and Flying Scotsman services with its presence and power, and was finally retired in 1963. It is now prominently displayed in the Great Hall of the National Railway Museum in York. On the cultural front, it achieved some additional cult status when it appeared on the cover of Britpop band Blur's 1993 album *Modern Life Is Rubbish*.

DUCHESS OF HAMILTON

Designer:	William Stanier
Built:	Crewe, Cheshire; 1938
Railway:	LMS (London, Midland and Scottish Railway)
Power:	Steam
Class:	Princess Coronation
Wheel arrangement:	4-6-2 Pacific (plus 6-wheel tender)
Number:	6229
Maximum speed:	114 miles per hour
Main service life:	Britain, West Coast Main Line
Current whereabouts:	National Railway Museum, York

Nigel Gresley didn't have it all his own way at LNER. While he was taking plaudits for the likes of *Mallard* running up and down the East Coast Main Line of Britain, his contemporary rival, William Stanier, was doing the same thing over on the West Coast

Main Line. Stanier's triumphs included the Princess Coronation Class, the most powerful (3,300 horsepower) passenger steam locomotive ever built. The *Duchess of Hamilton* was one of the few of that class to be streamlined, i.e. styled a lot like Gresley's *Mallard*, but Stanier took that step only under sufferance. Born in Swindon, Wiltshire, to a father who worked for the Great Western Railway, he preferred a no-nonsense approach to design and liked his locomotives to look like locomotives.

The streamlining was later removed from the *Duchess* and, after being taken out of service, she spent a period of ignominy as an exhibit at a Billy Butlin's Holiday Camp. Following a recent restoration, however, she now sits in the National Railway Museum in all her original streamlined glory, and right alongside *Mallard* at that. Just don't tell William Stanier.

20TH CENTURY LIMITED HUDSONS

Designer:	Paul W. Kiefer
Built:	Schenectady, New York; 1927–38
Railway:	New York Central Railroad
Power:	Steam
Class:	J-1, J-2, J-3
Wheel arrangement:	4-6-4 Hudson (plus 12-wheel tender)
Maximum speed:	100 miles per hour
Main service life:	New York to Chicago
Current whereabouts:	All scrapped

North American trains, from the early steam locomotives to the powerful diesels that replaced them, have always been massive and muscular. Once US train designers added streamlining and a large dose of the art-deco style so popular in the interwar years of the twentieth century, they started to look decidedly space age as well. From the cross-country Chiefs and Super Chiefs of the

Atchison, Topeka and Santa Fe Railway to the Zephyrs of the Chicago, Burlington and Quincy Railroad, they most certainly looked the part.

The most famous train of all was the New York Central Railroad's 20th Century Limited service, which ran along the Hudson Valley between New York and Chicago from 1902 until 1967, and which was for decades referred to as 'the greatest train in the world', at least by the American press.

The 20th Century Limited was powered for a long time by the iconic Hudson locomotives built by Alco (American Locomotive Company), and its passengers walked along a red carpet to board its equally iconic Pullman carriages. In 1934 the train became even more famous when it starred in a film also named after it, the screwball comedy *20th Century*, starring John Barrymore and Carole Lombard.

In the 1940s the Alco steam locomotives were replaced on the 20th Century Limited service by General Motors E7 'bulldog-nosed' diesels, and in this incarnation the train landed another big role, this time in the 1959 Alfred Hitchcock spy thriller *North by Northwest*, starring Cary Grant as 'regular guy on train mistaken for spy'.

UNION PACIFIC BIG BOY

Designer:	Otto Jabelmann
Built:	Schenectady, New York; 1941–44
Railway:	Union Pacific Railroad
Power:	Steam
Class:	4000
Wheel arrangement:	4-8-8-4 (plus 14-wheel tender)
Maximum speed:	80 miles per hour
Main service life:	Green River, Wyoming to Ogden, Utah
Current whereabouts:	Various US museums

After providing valuable support during World War Two by hauling huge numbers of troops, raw materials and military equipment to ports at both ends of the country, the 7,000-horsepower Big Boys made by Alco for the Union Pacific Railroad were put to use hauling freight. They hauled mile-long freight trains for 20 years over the Wasatch Mountains between Wyoming and Utah, each Big Boy notching up over a million miles in the process.

At 40 metres long from the cowcatcher at the front to the tender that carried 114,000 litres of water and 26,000 tons of coal at the back, each locomotive weighed as much as a hundred elephants (400 tons). The driving wheels alone were each 1.73 metres in diameter. If you want to feel really small, go and stand next to one of the eight that remain in railroad museums dotted around the USA (only 25 were ever made). Union Pacific has been restoring one of the Big Boys to operating condition at its steam shop in Cheyenne, Wyoming since 2014, with a projected completion date sometime in 2019.

SHINKANSEN SERIES O

Designer:	Hideo Shima
Built:	Japan; 1963–86
Railway:	West Japan Railways
Power:	Overhead electric
Class:	Series 0
Maximum speed:	130 miles per hour (140 miles per hour by 1986)
Main service life:	Tokyo to Osaka (initially)
Current whereabouts:	Various Japanese museums

When it was launched ahead of the 1964 Tokyo Olympics, the Shinkansen (meaning 'new trunk line') led the way in high-speed rail travel that didn't involve the shake, rattle and roll of the high-speed trains in Europe. Its revolutionary features included power to every single wheel axle, automatic braking, an in-cab track-signalling system, double-glazing, air conditioning and on-board telephones. Trains ran on new, dedicated tracks and, on average, arrived within 24 seconds of their schedule. The Shinkansen was dubbed the 'bullet train' because of its streamlined appearance and rounded nose.

Subsequent series of the Shinkansen might make the Series 0 look slow by comparison, but it will forever sit in the record books as the world's first superfast train. A total of 3,216 entered service, and the last one wasn't retired until 2008. Twenty-six of the trains are preserved in various Japanese museums, and there is also one in Britain, at the National Railway Museum in York.

TGV

Designer:	GEC-Alsthom (now Alstom)
Built:	France (initially); 1981 onwards
Railway:	SNCF (Société nationale des chemins de fer français)
Power:	Overhead electric
Maximum speed:	357 miles per hour
Main service life:	High-speed French and international routes
Current whereabouts:	Worldwide

French train builders used to let it all hang out, leaving their trains looking like Pompidou Centres on wheels, and perhaps this was one of the reasons they couldn't wait to get rid of steam once a sleek electric alternative became available. The *train à grande vitesse* (TGV) they came up with, however, was way beyond a simple upgrade of their previous efforts, going on to revolutionise rail travel the world over. Since the very first one went into service in 1981, TGVs have joined the bullet trains of Japan in setting the gold standard for high-speed rail travel. Here are just a few of the TGV's achievements:

▶ Holder of the Guinness world speed record (357 miles per hour) for conventional trains on a national rail system (as opposed to a test track) since 2007.

▶ For many years TGVs produced the fastest average start-to-stop speed of any scheduled service (*c.*175 miles per hour).

▶ A TGV broke the world speed record for an international journey when a Eurostar service carried the cast and producers of *The Da Vinci Code* from London to Cannes for the eponymous film festival in 2006. It covered the 883 miles in 7 hours 25 minutes.

▶ There are now well over 500 TGVs in France alone, including a double-decker version. Other countries have adopted the technology and now run their own models, so that TGVs can be admired across continental Europe and in parts of Asia and the Americas.

SHANGHAI MAGLEV

Designer:	Transrapid International
Built:	Siemens and ThyssenKrupp, Germany (trains only; the track was built by Chinese companies); 2004 onwards
Railway:	Chinese National Railways
Power:	Magnetic levitation

Maximum speed:	311 miles per hour (268 miles per hour when operated commercially)
Main service life:	Shanghai Airport to Shanghai Metro line
Current whereabouts:	Shanghai Airport to Shanghai Metro line

The Shanghai Maglev is the fastest train line in the world and was the first commercial service to operate by magnetic levitation at high speed. The German-built Transrapid 09 trains wrap their 'arms' around a T-shaped monorail to achieve forward propulsion and levitation through magnetic force alone. It is the first time in the history of rail travel that high-speed trains can run without making contact with their track. It takes less than 2 minutes for the 'floating bullet' trains to reach 200 miles per hour, with their 19-mile journey between Shanghai Pudong International Airport and the Longyang Road metro station taking a mere 7 minutes 20 seconds.

Whether maglev technology is the future of rail travel depends on whether business cases can justify the huge investment required to travel even faster than the already superfast 'traditional' high-speed electric trains that continue to spread around the world. Maglev trains feel a bit like a very expensive toy, but also a very impressive one.

PULLMAN CARRIAGES

Designer:	George Pullman
Built:	USA; 1863 onwards
Railway:	Most US railroads (initially)
Main service life:	US railroads and international Orient Express services
Current whereabouts:	Worldwide

I know a Pullman carriage can't go anywhere on its own, but I think it deserves a place in the train hall of fame on account of its longstanding reputation for providing rail travel at the sheer luxury end of the scale.

In 1865, industrialist George Pullman loaned the US government one of his recently built luxury sleeping cars as part of the cortege that conveyed the body of assassinated president Abraham Lincoln from Washington DC to his burial place at Springfield, Illinois. It proved to be a stroke of marketing genius as the millions who lined the route to pay their respects to Lincoln over a two-week period were also treated to their first glimpse of luxury rail travel. Orders then flooded in from railroad companies and the cars were thereafter named in Pullman's honour, becoming synonymous with the 'luxury hotel on wheels' status later enjoyed by the likes of the Orient Express.

No expense was spared and only the finest crystal, silver, mahogany, black walnut and marble were considered good enough to meet the sleeping, observing and fine-dining needs of those passengers with enough money or prestige not to have to travel with ordinary folk, who, after all, could probably not be relied upon to dress properly for dinner. Service was always impeccable, and recruitment was never a problem in the early days when the market was awash with recently freed house slaves.

The carriages have starred in their own right in countless books and films, as apt settings for high-end spies like James Bond and high-end detectives like Hercule Poirot. They have also starred in real life as the bedrooms, offices and dining cars of the world's royal families, presidents, maharajas, spies and celebrities. The *Ferdinand Magellan* Pullman carriage that transported the US president was, between 1943 and 1958, the armour-plated, bullet-resistant, US-railroad equivalent of the Air Force One presidential plane.

WHAT'S IN A NAME?

We have seen how many individual locomotives and services were given personalised names. This was usually done for marketing purposes and also sometimes to give train builders and railway employees a sense that their trains 'belonged' to them. Naming conventions have been random affairs, different designers and railway companies each doing their own thing for each class of locomotive or each route. Locomotive names have been adopted from worthy subjects as wide-ranging as military regiments, commanders and battles, literature, royalty, animals, castles and stately homes, ships, planes, countries and cities, mythological creatures, planets, birds and many more besides. In fact, it's probably the only thing that Robin Hood, Yuri Gagarin and the Duchess of Hamilton have in common. Just occasionally, though, trains or routes have been given names that are a little more unusual or frivolous than the norm:

The Lunatic Express: the railway system that linked the interiors of Uganda and Kenya to the Indian Ocean. Completed in 1902, it gained the name on account of the dangerous working conditions of those who built it, which included tropical diseases, hostile tribes and the infamous man-eating lions of Tsavo, which pulled railway workers out of their carriages at night.

The Fish and **The Chips:** two complementary commuter services that run over the Blue Mountains between Sydney and Lithgow in Australia. The Fish got its name from a nineteenth-century Aussie train driver called John Herron, a big man who went by the nickname of The Big Fish. The Chips must have seemed a pretty obvious choice when another service was added to the line.

Lady Penelope: a fleet of locomotives once used by Virgin Trains to rescue broken-down trains around the British mainland were named after *Thunderbirds* characters. When they were handed over to Direct Rail Services (DRS) in 2012, they were all renamed except for the *Lady Penelope*, which was allowed to keep its pink nameplate after DRS agreed to make a donation to the Railway Children charity. The other nameplates were auctioned by Virgin to raise funds for the Alzheimer's Society.

TRAIN OF THOUGHT
JUMBO TRAIN

The longest and heaviest train ever recorded stretched out for more than 4.5 miles and weighed 95,000 tonnes, the equivalent of 27,000 fully grown elephants. The freight train consisted of eight diesel locomotives hauling 682 wagons loaded with iron ore over a distance of 175 miles to the huge harbour at Port Hedland in Western Australia. You didn't want to get stuck at the level crossing that day.

BRAND NEW STEAM TRAINS

In 2008, after 18 years of toil and £3 million of donations, the first new steam locomotive to be built since 1960 was completed by the A1 Steam Locomotive Trust at Darlington Locomotive Works in England. Numbered 60163 and named *Tornado*, it is a Peppercorn Class A1 4-6-2 Pacific steam locomotive, which is used to run special services on the mainline railways of Britain. Peppercorn locomotives were originally built in 1948–49 and were so named after their designer, Arthur Peppercorn, the last chief mechanical engineer of the London and North Eastern Railway.

Since 2009, *Tornado* has been used on a number of occasions to pull the Royal Train conveying Prince Charles and the Duchess of Cornwall to public engagements, with Prince Charles riding in the cab whenever he can.

In 2017, *Tornado* clocked up 100 miles per hour on a night test run on the East Coast Main Line, the first steam train to reach this speed since the 1960s. That success means that it is now certified to run commercially at a top speed of 90 miles per hour, which is important to prevent it from impacting on the timetables of faster electric trains on the mainline. In that same year, *Tornado* landed a role playing itself in the *Paddington 2* film, with some of the filming taking place in – you guessed it – London Paddington station (there are also some great shots of *Tornado* on the move).

A second locomotive is now under construction by the Trust, this time a P2 Class 2-8-2 Mikado along the lines of the six originals of that Gresley class introduced between 1934 and 1936. The first of the six Mikado originals built in 1934 was the famous 2001 *Cock o' the North*; the new Mikado is to be known as 2007 *Prince of Wales*. The rare 2-8-2 wheel arrangement is what made the originals the most powerful passenger steam locomotives in Britain at the time, because their eight driving wheels allowed them to haul 15 carriages up the steep gradients from Edinburgh to Aberdeen.

TORNADO TO THE RESCUE

In the winter of late 2009, the steam locomotive *Tornado* left modern train services with egg on their faces when it rescued passengers stranded after cold weather had disabled the Ashford to Dover electric rail. It dropped them off while running a Christmas special from London to Dover during a week in which Eurostar suffered three days of cancellations on its Channel Tunnel services. It must have been the wrong kind of cold for modern technology that week.

MONUMENTAL STATIONS

*The only way to be sure of catching a
train is to miss the one before it.*

G. K. CHESTERTON

The French government obviously didn't agree with English
writer G. K. Chesterton, because, in 1891, they ordered all
clocks inside stations to run 5 minutes later than standard Paris
Mean Time. In this way, they meant to increase the number of
passengers catching their train without missing the previous
one. I am not sure if it worked, but the system remained in
place until 1911.

Chesterton's fellow English writer E. M. Forster got it spot on
when he said that railway termini are 'our gates to the glorious
and the unknown', because railway stations today remain our
gateways to adventure and sunshine, to the major cities of the
world, and to many other glorious destinations besides.

Many railway stations are amongst the engineering and
architectural wonders of the modern age. From the early cathedrals
and temples to the railway gods, often built in the classical or Gothic
style, to the aesthetically inspiring modernity of today's builds and

rebuilds, some of them have a beauty that simply inspires travel. They are also amongst the most functional of the world's buildings, often serving simultaneously as transport arteries, shopping malls, newsagents and eateries catering to every taste.

Some railway stations are also iconic for reasons of history or geography, or for having served as memorable settings for important literature and films. Whatever the reason for their iconic status in our consciousness, we will look at a few of the most significant ones in this chapter.

KING'S CROSS

Location: London, England
Opened: 1852
Designers: Lewis and William Cubitt (brothers)

London King's Cross Station is the gateway to the East Coast Main Line to Scotland, which links the capitals of England and Scotland, and the erstwhile launch pad for the likes of *Flying Scotsman* and *Mallard*. It was built with two great arched train sheds, the shape of which remains visible at the front of the station today, separated by a huge clock tower.

In 2012, it had a significant internal makeover, which included a magnificent new roof designed by John McAslan that has been described as a 'reverse waterfall'. Perhaps it is appropriate, then, that the station also houses Platform 9¾, the magical gateway to the Hogwarts Express that conveyed Harry Potter and his friends to school and back.

The station is thought by some historians to be the site of Queen Boudicca's final battle against the Romans, and there have been suggestions that she is buried beneath. Her ghost is even reported to have been seen wandering the passageways around platforms 8–10.

An IRA bomb caused extensive damage and injured six people in 1973, and a fire that started when a wooden escalator caught fire in 1987 claimed 31 lives and injured a further 100. Many improvements to fire safety regulations in stations occurred as a result.

TRAIN OF THOUGHT
THE MAGIC OF KING'S CROSS STATION

A special Platform 9¾ sign, complete with luggage trolley embedded in a brick wall, has recently been moved away from the platforms to the concourse area at King's Cross so that fans can queue for their photo opportunity without getting in the way of commuters who want to travel in a more conventional manner.

J. K. Rowling even set the epilogue to *Harry Potter and the Deathly Hallows* at King's Cross Station, giving it the undoubted honour of being the final setting in the whole series of Harry Potter books. That's what you call fame.

ST PANCRAS INTERNATIONAL

Location:	London, England
Opened:	1868 (rebuilt 2007)
Designers:	William Henry Barlow (1868); Alastair Lansley (2007)

Built adjacent to King's Cross Station, Barlow's pointed-arch train shed for St Pancras was a daring single span of iron and glass, at the time the largest of its kind in the world. It reached a height of 30 metres and a width of 73 metres, dimensions which were ideal for locomotives to let off steam and smoke without choking everybody in the station to death. This was one of the main reasons that Barlow's design was subsequently copied around the world.

In 1873, the Midland Grand Hotel (currently the St Pancras Renaissance), designed by architect George Gilbert Scott, was opened as a Victorian-Gothic-Revival-style frontispiece to the station and has been a well-known London landmark ever since.

The station escaped a planned demolition in the 1960s, not least thanks to English poet Sir John Betjeman, a driving force behind the campaign mounted to save its original fabric and design. By 2007 the station had not just been saved and sympathetically renovated, it had been expanded to become the quite stunning modern hub for Eurostar services to the continent, thereby gaining its international suffix. A wonderful lifelike statue of Betjeman by sculptor Martin Jennings stands in the international terminal as a fitting tribute to the poet's efforts.

Other notable features of the station concourse include: *The Meeting Place*, a 9-metre statue by Paul Day commonly known as 'The Lovers', the bronze plinth of which depicts scenes from the station's history; a Yamaha piano, left behind by Elton John after a performance at the station in 2016 and available to anyone to play; the Dent clock, an exact replica of the one that got smashed during renovations in the 1970s; and a section of each of the five Olympic rings that hung in the station in 2012, since converted into seating (the station served as the terminus for the Olympic Javelin Shuttle service, a 7-minute shuttle between Central London and the Olympic Park).

TRAIN OF THOUGHT
'PLEASE LOOK AFTER THIS BEAR. THANK YOU.'

London Paddington Station contains two solemn statues: one of Isambard Kingdom Brunel, the man who built the Great Western Railway (GWR) and the station that was built to serve it; the other of a World War One 'Tommy' on the memorial to the GWR employees who fell in that war.

The railway powers that be also showed they had a sense of humour when in 2000 they erected a statue of Paddington Bear in the station. The fictional bear created by Michael Bond in 1958 had, of course, been given the name 'Paddington' by the Brown family who found him at the station, just after he had arrived as a stowaway from deepest, darkest Peru, with the notice 'Please look after this bear. Thank you.' attached to his duffel coat.

RAILWAY MONOPOLY

Four of London's mainline railway stations feature on the British *Monopoly* board first introduced in 1936. They are, in clockwise order, Marylebone Station, Fenchurch Street Station, King's Cross Station and Liverpool Street Station, and they each cost a player £200 to buy. Waddingtons, the first manufacturer of the British version, was based in Leeds, which at the time was served by the London and North Eastern Railway (LNER). The LNER operated out of those four London stations, hence the reason for choosing them over the likes of Paddington, Victoria and Euston. In 2008, a

London Underground edition came out, so if four stations just aren't enough for you, knock yourself out with this one.

The US version (the game was, in fact, first produced in the USA in 1935) was set in and around Atlantic City, New Jersey, and has its railroad properties as Pennsylvania Railroad, B&O Railroad, Short Line, and Reading Railroad, each costing $200. In reality, the Short Line was in fact the Shore Fast Line, a streetcar line that served the city, and the B&O (Baltimore & Ohio) Railroad never served Atlantic City at all, although it was the parent company of the Reading Railroad and it did own some track in the area.

In 1994, new versions started to be produced that were set in other US cities, thereby enlisting a couple of hundred extra railroad stations to the *Monopoly* family. In 2003, the Hasbro toy company even chartered a special train from Chicago to Atlantic City so that it could host the US *Monopoly* National Championship on board.

Other rail connections over the years have included a steam locomotive token in certain Deluxe Editions; the introduction of little train depots that could be placed on the railway properties in some editions; and an entire Lionel Trains edition, thereby affording further immortality to the American toy train and model railroad company that was admitted in 2006 to the US National Toy Hall of Fame.

CHHATRAPATI SHIVAJI MAHARAJ TERMINUS

Location: Mumbai, India
Opened: 1888
Designer: Frederick William Stevens

Chhatrapati Shivaji Maharaj Terminus started life as the Victoria Terminus in what was then Bombay in the year following the Golden Jubilee of Queen Victoria, the ruling monarch of the United Kingdom and, of course, the Empress of India. Awash with domes, turrets, stone carvings and pointed arches built in yellow sandstone, granite and blue-grey basalt, it paid homage to George Gilbert Scott's hotel at St Pancras, but the Gothic Revival style was complemented by Mughal influences, an ensemble intended to capture a unique coming together of Western and Eastern styles. The entrance is flanked by the figures of a lion representing Britain and a tiger representing India. The red double-decker buses and Hindustan Ambassador taxis (based on the 1954 Morris Oxford) that stream past it to this day only add to the general air of nostalgia. Quite fittingly, the station has been listed since 2004 as a UNESCO World Heritage Site.

As soon as you step inside, however, you realise that this is no bygone relic. Used by more than three million commuters a day, and colour-splashed by a sea of saris, it is one of the great stations in which to stand still. It is also as good a place as any to hop on board and enjoy the unforgettable experience of a journey on Indian Railways.

The station has often appeared on screen, and in recent years starred as a major setting for *Slumdog Millionaire*, the 2008 Oscar-winning film directed by Englishman Danny Boyle.

The low point in the station's history came during the spate of terrorist attacks in Mumbai in 2008, when two men entered the main passenger hall and opened fire with AK-47 rifles and threw grenades, killing 58 people and injuring 104 others.

ESTACIÓN DE MADRID ATOCHA

Location: Madrid, Spain
Opened: 1851 (rebuilt 1892 and 1992)
Designers: Alberto Palacio (1892), Rafael Moneo (1992)

This station, named after the nearby basilica dedicated to Our Lady of Atocha, is like a beating heart that serves the national and international arteries that flow out from it in all directions.

After a fire had pretty much destroyed the original building, in 1892 Alberto Palacio adopted a style that made extensive use of wrought iron. He involved Frenchman Gustave Eiffel in the project, because apparently Monsieur Eiffel had some recent experience of his own in the building of a wrought-iron structure.

Exactly 100 years after the Palacio rebuild, the station then received the modern makeover that we see today, partly to accommodate Spain's growing high-speed rail network, and partly because it was time to get it ready for the twenty-first century. Inside today's station (designed by Rafael Moneo), the original concourse has become a vast plaza filled with tropical plants and flowers and ponds full of goldfish and rare turtles, as well as housing cafes, a shopping mall and a nightclub. One more poignant feature today is the memorial to the victims of the 2004 Madrid train bombings, which killed 192 and injured around 2,000 passengers on four separate commuter trains heading towards Atocha.

GARE DU NORD

Location:	Paris, France
Opened:	1846
Designer:	Jacques Hittorff

Serving northern France, Belgium, the Netherlands, Germany and Britain, the Gare du Nord is by far the busiest railway station in Europe, and the busiest in the world outside Japan. It is also one of the world's oldest stations, dating from the very early days of the railway. For that reason, it seems to have undergone a fairly constant renovation and expansion programme throughout its history. As the arrival point today of Eurostar trains from London (for which another extension was built in 1994), the station has become very familiar to millions of British business and leisure travellers.

The station, built in the Beaux Arts style, includes a huge 'triumphal arch' facade displaying 23 female statues, each representing a destination served by the station. They include allegorical representations of Berlin, Warsaw, Amsterdam, Vienna, Brussels and Frankfurt, with the figure representing Paris taking pride of place at the very top.

The Gare du Nord's screen appearances have included three blockbuster films already this century: action spy thriller *The Bourne Identity* (2002, Doug Liman), comedy heist *Ocean's Twelve* (2004, Steven Soderbergh), and the third Bourne film *The Bourne Ultimatum* (2007, Paul Greengrass). It was also where Mr Bean (Rowan Atkinson) arrived and suffered a misunderstanding with a taxi driver in the film comedy *Mr. Bean's Holiday* (2007, Steve Bendelack).

GARE DE LYON

Location:	Paris, France
Opened:	1900
Designer:	Marius Toudoire

Built for the Exposition Universelle (World's Fair) held in Paris in 1900, the Gare de Lyon was a *fin-de-siècle* triumph of belle époque sculpture and paintings. In addition to handling the increased capacity needed to support the fair, the station became a glorious setting for the arrival and departure of *Le Train Bleu*, the renowned service that carried the rich and famous to and from the French Riviera. The interior of the station is best known for the restaurant that bears the name of, and pays homage to, *Le Train Bleu*. Here, budget permitting, you can be fine-wined and dined while admiring the 30 scenes (by 30 different artists) of towns served by the erstwhile PLM (Paris–Lyon–Mediterranean Railway).

Times inside the restaurant have not changed much in over a hundred years, but outside is a different matter. Nowadays you can reach the Riviera on a high-speed train over the same length of time that you might spend on a leisurely lunch inside.

The station's screen roles have included the 2006 British ITV adaptation of the Agatha Christie thriller *The Mystery of the Blue Train*, and the romcom thriller *The Tourist* (2010, Florian Henckel von Donnersmarck), starring Johnny Depp and Angelina Jolie. Following his mishap with the taxi driver at Gare du Nord, it is also where Mr Bean turned up to sacrilegiously eat a langoustine whole at Le Train Bleu restaurant. *Sacré bleu!* (If you'll excuse the *jeu de mots*.)

TRAIN OF THOUGHT
MON DIEU! LA LOCOMOTIVE EST DANS LA PLACE.

On 22 October 1895, an express steam train from Granville in Normandy arrived at Gare Montparnasse in Paris. Unfortunately, it didn't stop there. Smashing through the buffers and across the concourse, it exited through a large first-floor window and ended up nose-first on the square below the station. Fortunately, the passenger carriages remained within the station. The photographs taken of the 'hanging' locomotive have been widely reproduced, and a replica of the scene has even been built at a theme park in Brazil.

GRAND CENTRAL TERMINAL

Location: New York City, New York, USA
Opened: 1913
Designers: Reed and Stem (overall design); Warren and Wetmore (Beaux Arts style)

Built in the Beaux Arts style, Grand Central today has more platforms than any other station in the world (44). It features two massive marbled staircases; a huge, blue-green astronomical painting on the main concourse ceiling; a facade sporting many classical statues (perhaps influenced by the style of the Gare du Nord in Paris) and a giant Tiffany clock; and the famous four-faced brass clock on top of the information booth that serves as a meeting point. The station survived a demolition threat in the 1960s and 1970s, with former First Lady Jacqueline Kennedy Onassis and architect Philip Johnson influential in getting the building designated a US National Historic Landmark.

There is so much to see and do inside the terminal that you can spend hours there without ever getting bored, even if you have nowhere to travel to. Work up an appetite by wandering around the myriad shops or food market, try a cocktail at the ultra-smart Campbell Bar, follow up with some oysters at the Grand Central Oyster Bar & Restaurant, then move on to a juicy steak at Michael Jordan's The Steak House. There is also an indoor tennis area.

If you're on a budget, have some free fun instead at the whispering gallery on the dining concourse, where low, ceramic arches will carry your whispered sayings around the dome of the curved ceiling as if you had almost shouted them. From November through to January each year, there is also a free model railway to delight railroad enthusiasts of all ages.

Even if you haven't been to Grand Central, you probably think you have, because, like so many Manhattan landmarks, the station has been appearing on your television and cinema screens since forever. Such saturated screen coverage probably accounts for the fact that Grand Central is one of the most-visited tourist attractions in the world, and most of those tourists never get on a train.

UNION STATION, WASHINGTON

Location: Washington DC, USA
Opened: 1907 (renovated 1988)
Designer: Daniel Burnham (renovation by Benjamin Thompson Associates)

The site of Amtrak's headquarters today, Union Station in DC was the world's biggest station when it opened (if you laid the Washington Monument on its side, it would fit inside). It originally housed a Turkish bath, a bowling alley and a mortuary. It was a masterpiece of the Beaux Arts style, modelled on the

Arch of Constantine and the Baths of Caracalla and Diocletian in Rome, a fitting setting for the several presidential inauguration balls to have been held at the station. Little expense was spared and marble, gold leaf and granite were amongst the materials used. The architect Daniel Burnham was following the tradition, which had started with London Euston in 1837, of treating the entrance to a major station as a triumphal arch.

A 1988 renovation was respectful of the original style but also reflected the cultural changes that had taken place in the USA since 1907, with parking for 1,500 cars, a nine-screen cinema and a multitude of cafes, bars, restaurants and shops taking the place of the Turkish bath, bowling alley and mortuary.

Note: A 'union station' was so-called because more than one railroad company had agreed to operate from it. In the case of Washington DC, the railroad companies that joined together in 1907 were the Baltimore and Ohio Railroad and the Pennsylvania Railroad.

UNION STATION, LOS ANGELES

Location: Los Angeles, California, USA
Opened: 1939
Designers: John and Donald Parkinson (father and son)

The style of this station exudes an almost spiritual air, its white bell tower reminiscent of California's mission halls. Its architects are said to have included elements of art deco, mission revival, Dutch colonial revival, Spanish-Colonial, Navajo and streamline moderne, and so it almost beggars belief that its beauty seems to lie in the apparent simplicity of the finished product. Set within charming landscaped gardens and cool courtyards, there can be few more relaxing spaces in which to await a train. Terracotta, marble and steel were all made use of to keep passengers cool in this refuge from the baking Californian sun. It was built to host the great trains of the Southern Pacific, Union Pacific and Santa Fe Railroads, including the famed Super Chief service of the Santa Fe, also known as the 'Train of the Stars' because of all the celebrities it ferried between Los Angeles and Chicago – the Super Chief was the first all-Pullman sleeping car train in the USA. The station will be known in future as much for the part it plays as a hub in the California High-Speed Rail Link.

Not surprisingly, given its proximity to Hollywood, the station has been used as a setting in scores of movies, including romantic drama *The Way We Were* (1973), comedy thriller *Silver Streak* (1976), sci-fi thriller *Blade Runner* (1982) and war epic *Pearl Harbor* (2001).

BERLIN HAUPTBAHNHOF

Location:	Berlin, Germany
Opened:	2006
Designer:	Meinhard von Gerkan

After the Berlin Wall came down in 1989, Germany set about reconnecting its rail network and chose the site of the old Lehrter Stadtbahnhof in Berlin to be developed as the hub. When the striking Berlin Hauptbahnhof finally opened in 2006, it was hailed as an architectural wonder and a proud symbol of east/west reunification. Perhaps somewhat bizarrely in the political circumstances, the architects adopted what they described as French Renaissance style, but I have to say that the colossal steel and glass structure strikes me as more twenty-first century than medieval chateau.

The station is also something of an engineering triumph, involving a number of perpendicular levels, the highest at 10 metres above ground and the lowest at 15 metres below, with a diversion of the River Spree thrown in for good measure.

Tracks run on two of the levels, handling up to 1,800 trains and 350,000 passengers each day.

HELSINKI CENTRAL STATION

Location:	Helsinki, Finland
Opened:	1919
Designer:	Eliel Saarinen

With independence from Soviet Russia in the air, and the music of Jean Sibelius in full flow, Finnish architects enjoyed a hitherto unimaginable freedom of expression in the early twentieth century. Nowhere is this more evident than in Saarinen's granite-clad station, arguably the Finnish capital city's most striking landmark. Two pairs of giant lantern-bearing statues, one pair on either side of the main entrance, dominate its facade and look especially impressive when the huge spherical lanterns are lit at night. Along with an even more gigantic clock tower, they positively loom over the surrounding area.

The station continues to impress today, not just architecturally, but also from a service point of view. Trains run on time from its 19 platforms, the food and service within is good, and the building is spotlessly clean. Over 200,000 passengers a day make it the country's most-visited building.

MOSCOW KAZANSKAYA STATION

Location:	Moscow, Russia
Opened:	1864 (rebuilt 1913–40)
Designer:	Alexey Shchusev (rebuild)

The citadel-style Kazanskaya Station sits on Komsomolskaya Square, along with Leningradsky and Yaroslavsky Stations.

It is Moscow's largest station and trains from here serve Ryazan, Yekaterinburg and Kazan (Russian terminals are generally named after the main destination their trains travel to), and Shchusev's rebuild was modelled on the Söyembikä Tower within the Kazan Kremlin. You can also begin a Trans-Siberian journey here, but not before enjoying some food and a vodka or five under the gloriously over-the-top ceiling of the station restaurant – it would not look out of place at the Bolshoi. Various styles compete for your attention around the entire station, from rococo to art nouveau.

STESEN KERETAPI KUALA LUMPUR

Location:	Kuala Lumpur, Malaysia
Opened:	1910
Designer:	Brigadier General Arthur Benison Hubback

You could be forgiven for missing this station entirely (and I did, at least initially) because, from the outside, it looks more like a Raj-style pavilion than a railway station. Apparently, at the time it was built, that well-known architectural mix of Neo-Moorish/Mughal/Indo-Saracenic with the odd dollop of Western influence was all the rage (think lots of arches and minaret-like domes).

After a lot of its traffic was moved to nearby Kuala Lumpur Sentral, much of the station was converted to a railway museum in 2007, with many of the original station's furnishings now displayed on the main concourse and platform, and within the on-site Heritage Station Hotel.

KANAZAWA STATION

Location:	Ishikawa Province, Honshu Island, Japan
Opened:	1898 (current building completed in 2005)
Designer:	Ryuzo Shiroe (current building)

Entirely elevated above street level, the futuristic architecture of Kanazawa Station includes the Montenashi (Welcome) Dome, which resembles a huge glass umbrella, and the equally huge Tsuzumi-mon Gate, a wooden 'temple shrine' gateway that symbolises traditional Japanese hand drums (tsuzumis). Outside is a fountain that changes its flow pattern so as always to digitally display the current time. The addition of a Shinkansen (bullet train) link, which puts the city within 2 hours 30 minutes of Tokyo, has further helped to put Kanazawa firmly on the Japanese railway map.

ANTWERPEN-CENTRAAL STATION

Location: Antwerp, Belgium
Opened: 1905
Designers: Louis Delacenserie/Clement van Bogaert

If you like neo-baroque palaces, try Antwerpen-Centraal. Nicknamed the 'Railway Cathedral' on account of its huge size, iron-and-glass vaulted ceiling and over-the-top interior, it was kitted out with 20 different kinds of marble and stone. An award-winning reconstruction in the early part of this century has converted what was previously a terminus to a through-station on four levels, but without losing any of the original splendour. Often voted one of the most beautiful stations in the world, the magnificence of its architecture is described in some detail in the opening of the 2001 book *Austerlitz*, the final novel of German writer W. G. Sebald.

The station went viral in 2009 when a flash mob of 200 dancers of all ages staged a choreographed performance of 'Do-Re-Mi' from *The Sound of Music* to advertise a Belgian TV talent show, *Op zoek naar Maria*, their version of the BBC talent show *How Do You Solve a Problem Like Maria?*

HUA HIN STATION

Location: Hua Hin, Thailand
Opened: 1910 (redesigned 1925)
Designer: Prince Purachatra Jayakara (1925 rebuild)

One of Thailand's oldest, Hua Hin Station was built to allow the king and his family access to their nearby summer palace. The little pavilion-like station is a photographer's paradise on account of its exotic architecture, well-maintained gardens and colourful people-watching opportunities. The Royal Waiting Room looks particularly delicate, which isn't surprising seeing as it started life as a royal pavilion in the grounds of Sanam Chandra Palace at Nakhon Pathom before being moved to the station in 1967 to allow the royal family to relax while they were waiting to go home. Train enthusiasts can also enjoy the retired US-built 2-8-2 Mikado steam locomotive that is housed at the station. On the odd occasion, you can also admire the Eastern & Oriental Express as it passes through on its way from Bangkok to Kuala Lumpur and Singapore.

STAZIONE DI VENEZIA SANTA LUCIA

Location: Venice, Italy
Opened: 1861 (with 1952 rebuild)
Designers: Angiolo Mazzoni/Virgilio Vallot/Paul Perilli (1952 rebuild)

State architect Mazzoni first planned the current station in 1924 but, in true Italian fashion, it took three architects, countless designs and redesigns, and almost 30 years to complete. It is one of the few modernist buildings to overlook the Grand Canal, but look out for the Venetian lions that at least decorate the flanks of its facade.

Because it sits on the Grand Canal in the Cannaregio district, train passengers spill straight out of the station onto one of the wonders of the world, having crossed the *Ponte della Libertà*, the 2-mile causeway from the mainland, only moments before. Location, location, location!

Whether you set out from London on the Orient Express, or from Milan on a high-speed train, or from a local station across on the mainland, there are not many train journeys that deliver you straight into the heart of a completely different world to that which you left behind. 'Just add water' is perhaps what it should say on the train ticket.

GREAT RAILWAY ACHIEVEMENTS

British by design

Keeping alive a long British tradition that started with Brunel's groundbreaking nineteenth-century design for London Paddington, British architect Norman Foster has in more recent times designed a new roof for Dresden Hauptbahnhof in Germany; a new high-speed rail terminus in Florence, Italy; the Canary Wharf station on the London Underground; and four stations on the Mecca–Medina high-speed line in Saudi Arabia. In 2017, his firm was also awarded a contract to design seven new stations for the Sydney Metro extension that is due to start operating in 2024.

DUNEDIN RAILWAY STATION

Location: Dunedin, South Island, New Zealand
Opened: 1906
Designers: George Troup

The eclectic revived Flemish renaissance style of the building earned the station's architect the nickname 'Gingerbread George'. The light and dark effect was achieved by using layers of dark basalt and light Oamaru stone, with some pink granite thrown in to support the colonnade out front. The roof consists of terracotta shingles from Marseille topped with copper-domed cupolas. However gaudy all that might sound, the overall effect is actually quite pleasing to the eye, as is the mosaic floor within.

The station has lost most of its traffic since it opened and it now serves as a station on what has largely become a sightseeing line for tourists.

TRAIN OF THOUGHT
EELS AND ANTS

If you want a wonderful bird's-eye view of a railway station, buy a ticket for the View from the Shard, which will take you in a lift to Level 72 of one of London's most iconic skyscrapers. You will be able to gaze down on what look like lots of eels slithering in and out of London Bridge Station far below, and marvel at the thousands of ants that the eels seem to disgorge upon arrival, before gorging on lots more before setting off again.

You will also be able to see at a glance how the recent rebuilding project has brought London's oldest railway terminus bang up-to-date, including a single concourse serving all 15 platforms that is bigger than the football pitch at Wembley Stadium.

GREAT TRAIN JOURNEYS

There's something about the sound of a train
that's very romantic and nostalgic and hopeful.
PAUL SIMON

It was while waiting in a railway station, with a ticket to his destination, that Paul Simon penned the lyrics in 1964 for 'Homeward Bound', Simon and Garfunkel's second hit song. The railway station in question was Widnes (then in Lancashire, now in Cheshire) and the train he was waiting for was the early-morning milk train down to London, which was indeed his home at that time. The Widnes to London milk train was probably never one of the world's great railway journeys, but that particular route for Simon was more about the end point. There are, however, many railway trips that are worth taking as much for the journey as the destination.

Great railway journeys abound the world over, and always will. They afford the opportunity to travel on trains of all shapes and sizes and ages, from those driven by steam to those propelled by magnetic levitation. They cover their respective territories on track gauges suitable for their terrain, whether pastoral or desert, through mountains or across or under water. What makes a railway journey great is a matter of subjective opinion, and it would be impossible to cover them all in anything less than an encyclopaedia, so I will do what everyone else does and select a number of personal favourites, some of which I have already enjoyed, the rest of which remain firmly on my bucket list.

But let us start by paying homage to the two men who first recognised the greatness of the railway excursion, and who first alerted the world to its very many possibilities: George Bradshaw and Thomas Cook.

NOW, THAT'S WHAT YOU CALL A RAILWAY GUIDE, BY GEORGE!

Lancashire-born George Bradshaw produced the world's first compilation of railway times in 1839. He made the times easier to follow by setting them out in a table, a revolutionary concept that we take for granted today as a 'timetable'.

As the railways of Britain and Europe grew, so did the publications of his timetables and travel guides to service the burgeoning tourism industry. Their reach ultimately extended further east to include, by 1903, the magnificently titled *Bradshaw's Through Routes to the Capitals of the World, and Overland Guide to India, Persia and the Far East*. Bradshaw had died prematurely of cholera in 1853 at the age of 52, but the books that bore his name continued to be published until 1961.

His name became synonymous with rail travel, to the extent that travellers referred to their 'Bradshaw' as opposed to their 'timetable', in the same way that people often still refer to their 'Hoover' as opposed to their 'vacuum cleaner'. He even made it as a verb during World War Two when 'to Bradshaw' meant to navigate an aeroplane along the course of a railway line below.

Although current Bradshaw's guides are no longer available to us as we plan our own great railway journeys, the reproductions that we can buy today of some of the old ones remain a fascinating insight into a bygone age, with some descriptions that might take you by surprise if you were to see them in a guidebook today:

Hastings (East Sussex):
A very efficient substitute for a trip to Madeira.

Hull (East Yorkshire):
Seems to rise like Venice from amidst the sea.

'COOK'S TOURS'

Englishman Thomas Cook was a former Baptist minister who had taken the no-alcohol pledge and set about encouraging others to do the same. In 1841, he arranged a rail excursion for 540 travellers to attend a temperance rally, convincing the railway company that each should be charged a flat fee including the cost of their food on the day. Encouraged by his success, he set about arranging rail excursions for pleasure, and the package deal was born. Once he could no longer cope with going along as guide on every package holiday he arranged, he came up with the idea of inclusive independent travel, setting his clients up with all the bookings, documents and information they needed to travel the world's railways (and steamers) by themselves. The concept of visiting a number of destinations according to a single itinerary within a confined amount of time became popularly known as a 'Cook's Tour', something which effectively remains on offer today from the Thomas Cook Group, which is a direct descendant of the original company.

THE MAN IN SEAT SIXTY-ONE

Our twenty-first-century version of George Bradshaw's guides is the travel website www.seat61.com, which focuses almost entirely on train-based travel around the world. It is run by Englishman Mark Smith, an ex-rail-industry manager, and has won numerous awards for its advice about the best routes, times and costs for travelling from just about anywhere to just about anywhere else. The name of the website derives from his own favourite seat when travelling first class to Europe on Eurostar, as do the accompanying books based on his own travels.

Starting in the Scottish Highlands, and finishing at Machu Picchu, let us now have a look at just some of the great railway journeys available to us today. George Bradshaw and Thomas Cook would have loved them all. The Man in Seat Sixty-One still does.

WEST HIGHLAND LINE (SCOTLAND)

Not just generally accepted to be the most scenic railway journey in Britain, the West Highland Line is regularly voted the best railway journey in the world. If you are setting out from London, the first part of your journey will be to Fort William, at the foot of Ben Nevis in the Scottish Highlands, on the 9 p.m. scheduled Caledonian Sleeper (every night of the year except Saturdays), also known as the 'Deerstalker'. Enjoy haggis, neeps and tatties washed down with a malt or two from the on-board bar before retiring to dream of the scenery that will greet you over breakfast.

An extension of the West Highland Line takes you out west from Fort William to Mallaig, opposite the Isle of Skye. The three options for travelling this route are: the run-of-the-mill scheduled service; the Jacobite steam service that runs in the summer and has in recent years been immortalised as the Hogwarts Express in the Harry Potter films; and the luxurious Royal Scotsman service, which runs Highland tours in the summer out of Edinburgh.

Mile for mile, the Royal Scotsman is the most expensive railway service in the world and you will need to dress in your stateroom for dinner while agonising over which of the 30 malt whiskies to try next. Whether you blow your savings on the Royal Scotsman or take the local train, the scenery will be the same: mile after mile of spectacular mountains, lochs and deer-filled glens.

GREAT RAILWAY ACHIEVEMENTS

Glenfinnan Viaduct

Known to millions of Harry Potter fans as the viaduct that the Hogwarts Express winds across, the Glenfinnan Viaduct is one of the engineering wonders of the West Highland Line. It was built in 1898 by 'Concrete Bob' (Sir Robert McAlpine) at a time when poured-concrete construction was positively revolutionary. Spanning 380 metres, the 21 semi-circular arches reach a height of 30 metres, offering rail passengers quite spectacular views of Loch Shiel and beyond. In recognition of McAlpine's genius, the viaduct is depicted on the back of a Bank of Scotland £10 note. The Harry Potter production team based for nine years, on and off, in the tiny village of Glenfinnan must have got through a few of them. When a new polymer version of the note was issued in 2017, the viaduct remained on the back of it, but now it had the addition of a train crossing over it, hauled by an LMS Stanier 'Black Five' 4-6-0 steam locomotive. The Black Five was an iconic London, Midland and Scottish locomotive that once saw a lot of service on the West Highland Line and, therefore, on the Glenfinnan Viaduct.

SETTLE-CARLISLE LINE (ENGLAND)

This 72-mile line between Settle in North Yorkshire and Carlisle in Cumbria offers wonderful views as it takes in the more remote moors of the Yorkshire Dales, one of England's National Parks, and the North Pennines, a designated Area of Outstanding Natural Beauty.

The terrain was truly difficult to build through when the line was constructed in the nineteenth century, and 14 tunnels and 21 glorious viaducts, including the longest at Ribblehead and the highest at Smardale, were needed to cross the moors and cut through the Pennines. Dent Station in Cumbria is the highest mainline station in Britain, at 350 metres above sea level.

British Rail twice failed in its attempts to close the line, in the 1960s and 1980s, and the line is going strong today, not only as a mainline passenger and freight route, but also as a popular through route for steam excursions (which don't, however, stop at any of the stations on the line). Annual passenger numbers have grown to over a million since the dark days of threatened closures, and eight closed stations have since reopened and been given makeovers. After part of the line was closed following a landslip in 2016, the reopening of the full line in 2017 was celebrated with the first regular scheduled mainline service to be run with a steam engine in Britain for almost half a century. The engine given that honour was Britain's newest steam locomotive, *Tornado*. A special service was also run to commemorate the reopening by Britain's most famous steam locomotive, *Flying Scotsman*.

Michael Portillo was instrumental in saving the line from certain closure in 1989 when, as transport minister, he convinced Margaret Thatcher to refuse the second British Rail application to shut it down. He has since said that he considers the part he played in saving the railway line to be one of his greatest achievements in politics.

TRAIN OF THOUGHT
THE FORMER FUTURE BRITISH PRIME MINISTER

Michael Portillo was for many years a Conservative Party politician, a loyal supporter of Margaret Thatcher who went on to serve as a cabinet minister under John Major. He was once tipped to become leader of the party himself and, by extension, a future prime minister. With that kind of hardcore political stuff on your curriculum vitae, you probably don't aspire to be everyone's cup of tea, so it has come as something of a surprise that Michael Portillo, since retiring from politics, has gone on to become one of Britain's favourite TV and radio presenters.

His passion for rail travel was reinforced while serving as transport minister, so perhaps it is less of a surprise that his many programmes in recent years have included the ever-popular *Great British Railway Journeys* and *Great Continental Railway Journeys*. His unbounded enthusiasm for rail travel, his easy connection with people from all walks of life and his I'll-have-a-go-at-anything presenting style have won him many fans, and the journeys he describes are inspiring a new generation of travellers to take to the rails.

GLACIER EXPRESS (SWITZERLAND)

Glacier Express is something of a misnomer, really, as the train takes 8 hours to cover the 180 miles between Zermatt and St Moritz in the Swiss Alps, but you have to concede that it's probably a bit quicker than walking across 291 ravines and scrambling along 91 mountainsides to reach your ski resort. The track is narrow-gauge (including the longest narrow-gauge tunnel in the world), switching to rack-and-pinion when the going gets tough, and tunnel-and-pass-over-yourself spirals when the going gets even tougher. Creature comforts on board the Glacier Express include warmth, good food in lavish dining cars, tilting wine glasses, and glass roofs for your panoramic viewing pleasure. If snow and ice aren't your things, the summer views still live up to that Alpine jigsaw you put together as a kid.

JUNGFRAU RAILWAY (SWITZERLAND)

If you always wanted to climb the Eiger, one of the most difficult and dangerous mountains in the world, but feel less keen about risking your life in the process, you could always scale the infamous north face by train.

The cogwheel, metre-gauge Jungfrau Railway in Switzerland runs from the picturesque mountain village of Kleine Scheidegg through tunnels that have been carved into the Eiger and Mönch mountains to arrive 5.6 miles and 50 minutes later at Jungfraujoch, Europe's highest railway station at 3,454 metres above sea level. There you can relax in a restaurant or coffee bar while taking in the breathtaking views of nearby glaciers and peaks. There is also a post office (Europe's highest), souvenir shops, an 'ice palace' and an observatory with a viewing deck – which you have to take a lift up to, as if you weren't high enough already! Step outside and the views will literally take your breath away because, until you have acclimatised to the altitude, it will feel as if somebody is trying to insert an ice cube into your throat.

If you can't get to Switzerland, you can still see the train and its stunning locations by watching the acclaimed 1975 film *The Eiger Sanction*, the assassination thriller starring and directed by Clint Eastwood.

ANY TRAIN TO THE SOUTH OF FRANCE

Whether you choose a superfast TGV or something a little slower, the best train journey to take in France is from Paris down to the

French Riviera. In a matter of hours, you will enjoy a complete change of terrain, temperature and light: it is not uncommon on that journey to remove at least one layer of clothing and don your sunglasses. You can't 'sense' a journey like that travelling by plane, which is one of the reasons the French have managed to entice many domestic plane passengers back onto the tracks in recent years. The scenery is pretty spectacular at times, too, not least because you spend half the journey crossing the spectacular Massif Central.

OSLO-BERGEN LINE (NORWAY)

If oxblood wooden cabins dotted around crystal-clear fjords float your (Viking) boat, and you like the idea of travelling across plateaux devoid of human activity, you will love the entire range of scenery along the Oslo–Bergen Line. Highlights along the 310-mile route between Norway's capital and its scenic second city (which takes around 6 hours 30 minutes to travel) include year-round snow views above the treeline and, just like the West Highland Line (see above), a station so remote that there are no roads to or from it. This is the territory in which Scott's team chose to train prior to their ill-fated expedition to the Antarctic in 1910–12, and which the makers of the 1980 Star Wars epic *The Empire Strikes Back* chose to represent the icy planet of the Hoth system.

The line is also popular for the opportunity to alight at Myrdal and take the spectacular branch-line excursion down to Flåm, which drops 863 metres over 12.5 miles. It is the steepest standard-gauge railway in Europe and comes with an astonishing view of the Sognefjord (Norway's longest and deepest fjord) as the train twists slowly down the mountain.

ORIENT EXPRESS (EUROPE AND SOUTH EAST ASIA)

Step back in time and party like it's 1899, or the roaring 1920s, or any other time that takes your fancy since the Compagnie Internationale des Wagons-Lits started to run its services from Paris in 1883. The current incarnation of the Orient Express continues to evoke an age when the style and romance of the journey were at least as important as the destination, and the art deco opulence of your carriage was up to the standard of the luxury hotel you were headed for. Sparkling crystal, polished wood and plush fabrics positively abound, and the dress code for dinner is sophisticated elegance. Dinner is always served on time, because long gone are the days when an irritating Belgian detective was allowed to hold up the next meal in order to have a denouement in the dining car, or when the train had to move to a siding to count the number of passengers who had not yet been murdered.

The European cities you can still travel to in such luxury today include Paris, Venice, Stockholm and Vienna. If you would prefer something a little sultrier, the Eastern and Oriental Express allows you to have a similar (but smart-casual) experience on the 1,200-mile Bangkok–Kuala Lumpur–Singapore line. Travelling in Japanese-built coaches that once plied their trade in New Zealand (on the Silver Star service), your views from the train will include many more rubber plantations and paddy fields than you are likely to see en route to Vienna.

MAHARAJAS' EXPRESS (RAJASTHAN, INDIA)

Of all India's magnificently named luxury train services (which include the Royal Rajasthan on Wheels, the Golden Chariot, the Deccan Odyssey and the Palace on Wheels), the Maharajas' Express claims to be the most luxurious and is surely the most magnificently named. As the winner of many world travel awards, it is also one of the most expensive luxury trains on the planet.

One of its tours, the Heritage of India, provides a week-long trip from Mumbai to Delhi that takes in the lakes and palaces of Udaipur; the blue city of Jodhpur; the pink city of Jaipur; Ranthambore for a bit of tiger-spotting; and Agra for the Taj Mahal, the world's most famous monument to love. When you are not being struck dumb by the destinations, you spend your time being struck dumb by the opulence of the train itself, especially if you can afford around £20,000 per person for the presidential suite, which takes up an entire carriage in order to accommodate your private sitting-cum-dining room and your en-suite master and guest bedrooms. If you're going to take the Maharajas' Express, you might as well live like them while you're on board. If you're happy to slum it in the Deluxe Cabin, though, you can make the same journey for the relatively paltry sum of £5,000. You'll still enjoy personal valet service, your own en-suite luxury cabin and the smooth journey you would expect from a train with pneumatic suspension.

'TOY TRAIN' TO DARJEELING (INDIAN HIMALAYAS)

Staying within India, but at the other end of the financial scale from the Maharajas' Express, you can take the Darjeeling Himalayan Railway, popularly known as the 'Toy Train', for a fistful of rupees. Completed in 1881, the line climbs 2,225 metres up into the Himalayas from New Jalpaiguri in West Bengal. It is one of the narrow-gauge mountain railways designed by the British to reach the relative cool of their hill stations in the summer (in this case, to escape the fierce heat of Calcutta, now Kolkata).

It conquered 50 miles of mountainous terrain with frequent loops, spirals, zigzags and hideously sharp curves, and needed the narrowest of narrow gauges (0.6 metres) and the smallest of tank engines (B Class 0-4-0ST) to achieve the tortuous climb, although nowadays small diesel engines also take their turn. Surprisingly for a mountain railway, there are no tunnels, which means that you get to enjoy the scenery all the way up, including close-ups of hill towns and villages and, of course, the world-famous tea plantations. Clouds permitting, you may also be rewarded with a panoramic view that includes Mounts Everest and Kangchenjunga, two of the world's three highest mountains.

The journey today may continue to evoke the bygone era of the Raj, but it also remains a very Indian experience and it is all the better for it.

BLUE TRAIN AND ROVOS RAIL (SOUTH AFRICA)

If endless savannah, wild animals and stunning sunsets are more your thing, hop on board the Blue Train (not to be confused with the French Riviera version) for its sedate 27-hour, 994-mile journey across South Africa between Pretoria and Cape Town. Often heralded as the most lavish train in the world, its sapphire-blue carriages are at the luxury end of the scale. Services include 24/7 on-call personal butlers and strictly formal dining in plush surroundings, although the recommended dress code for lunch is scaled down to 'elegant casual'. If you haven't blown your entire savings on the trip itself, fear not, you can easily blow the rest in the on-board jewellery boutique.

If you want to make the journey at an even more sedate pace, but at the same standard of luxury, rival company Rovos Rail takes an extra day and night to cover the distance in restored Rhodesia Railways coaches. The company also offers an astonishing safari route into Namibia (including the Kalahari Desert and the Etosha Pan) and an epic route from Cape Town to Dar-es-Salaam in Tanzania, taking in Botswana, Zimbabwe (including Victoria Falls) and Zambia along the way. Rovos Rail is a family-owned company, and Rovos is a contraction of Rohan Vos, the head of the family who founded it in 1989.

Both companies claim to run one of the most luxurious train services in the world, and they're probably both not far wrong.

Note: If your budget doesn't stretch to around £900 for the one-way trip on either of the luxury services, you can journey between Cape Town and Johannesburg on the public Shosholoza Meyl sleeper service for around £40 including meals. The trains are perfectly comfortable and the staggeringly beautiful scenery will be the same, making this the biggest rail-travel bargain you are ever likely to strike in your entire life.

TRANS-SIBERIAN RAILWAY (RUSSIA AND CHINA)

Since 1904, the main line of the Trans-Siberian Railway out of Moscow has covered 5,772 miles to deliver passengers to stations all the way to Vladivostok on the Sea of Japan. It is Russia's main transport artery, carrying 30 per cent of the country's export freight and most of its domestic passenger traffic. If you want the ultimate first-class tourist experience, attended night and day by smiling, deferential staff, try the private Golden Eagle service. If you consider yourself more traveller than tourist, however, you might prefer that most Russian of experiences, the state-run Rossiya ('Russia') service, where smiles and deference can be harder to find. Either way, the journey takes eight days and crosses seven time zones in conquering the icy wastes of southern Siberia. In terms of scenery, think *Doctor Zhivago* and your expectations should be met.

There is also a Moscow–Beijing alternative on the Trans-Siberian Railway, the Trans-Mongolian Express, which is serviced by a Chinese train. It uses the same line as the Moscow–Vladivostok service until it drops down from Siberia to travel through Mongolia and the Gobi Desert on its way to the Chinese capital. What this means is that you only have to change twice (in Paris and Moscow) to travel from London St Pancras to Beijing by train. I don't know about you, but that certainly boggles my mind.

SHINKANSEN SERVICES (JAPAN)

If it's an adrenalin rush you're after, or if you're just in a hurry to say you've been on one of the great railway journeys of the world, head straight to Japan. The bullet train is not so named for nothing, so don't be surprised if the experience feels more like a rocket launch than a train journey. There are many routes to choose from, including Tokyo to Kyoto. You'll feel as if you're on one of the faster rides at Disneyland, except you can't get off for 2 hours 20 minutes and during that time you'll have travelled 325 miles. The other, and probably the best, reason for choosing this route is that you get to see the iconic view of Mount Fuji from the train, though you'd better be quick if you want to get that classic selfie on the way past.

GHAN AND INDIAN PACIFIC (AUSTRALIA)

Although the line that sought to cross the vast Australian continent from top to bottom was begun in 1878, it wasn't until 2004 that the top part of the line, from Alice Springs to Darwin, was finally completed.

Until 1929, that final leg of the journey had been an Afghan camel ride between Alice Springs and Darwin, hence the name of the entire top-to-bottom train service today, the Ghan. Afghan camel riders had arrived in Australia in the nineteenth century to help the British find routes into the interior.

It takes the diesel locomotives around 50 hours to haul the stainless steel carriages across 1,852 miles of outback, more outback and even more outback between Adelaide and Darwin, with kangaroo-spotting the recommended way to while away the hours. If booking a package deal, the one optional excursion you might find difficult to resist is the overnight coach trip from Alice Springs to witness the glowing red sandstone of Uluru.

Of course, you can also cross Australia from side to side (the Trans-Australian Railway was completed as long ago as 1917) on the Indian Pacific service, so called because the journey takes you all the way from Perth, on the Indian Ocean, to Sydney, on the Pacific. You will need an extra night to cross the continent this way, because the route, at 2,704 miles, is nearly a thousand miles longer than the Ghan, and includes the longest dead-straight stretch of track in the world, running for 297 miles across the arid Nullarbor Plain (Nullarbor is from the Latin *nullus arbor*, meaning 'no tree').

TRAIN OF THOUGHT
GETTING THE HANG OF RAIL TRAVEL

In 2009, a 19-year-old American tourist was left clinging to the outside of the Ghan after being locked out of the train at a stop in Port Augusta in South Australia. Two hours and 120 miles later, his screams were finally heard by a railway employee, who got the driver to stop the train.

AUCKLAND-WELLINGTON NORTHERN EXPLORER (NEW ZEALAND)

This is one of the world's epic rides, taking around 11 hours to cross the 423 miles of North Island that separates New Zealand's two largest cities. You won't get bored of the forever-changing scenery, which includes coastline, rivers, snow-capped mountains and volcanoes, lakes, viaducts, gorges, rainforest, lush farmland and thick bush. The KiwiRail carriages are clean, bright and comfortable, offering ample panoramas every mile of the way. A recorded commentary is also provided via free headphones, so you'll never have to wonder what it is you're looking at (unless you see some red deer for the first time in your life, but that probably won't throw you either, because they look like deer and they're red). Do look out for hobbit holes, because you will be passing through the territory used as the Shire in Middle-earth by Peter Jackson in *The Lord of the Rings* and *The Hobbit* movies.

ROCKY MOUNTAINEER (CANADA)

The most famous Rocky Mountaineer trip is the First Passage to the West, the route that runs over the original Canadian Pacific track between Vancouver and Banff. Even by Canadian standards the mountain scenery is hard to beat, and highlights, as you will know from every worldwide holiday brochure you have ever seen, include Banff and Lake Louise. The train cuts through the Rockies along the magnificently named Kicking Horse Canyon, one of the many places where you should keep your eyes open for bald eagles, grizzlies or maybe even Bigfoot himself. Unlike many other luxury trains, these only travel during daylight hours, with passengers overnighting instead in luxury hotels and thereby avoiding the irritation of squandering their savings on panoramic views of darkness.

Other stunning Rocky Mountaineer routes include the Whistler Sea to Sky Climb and the Coastal Passage (which also crosses the border to Seattle, Washington).

CALIFORNIA ZEPHYR AND TEXAS EAGLE (USA)

These Amtrak services, hauled by powerful diesel locomotives, seek to relive the glory days of America's transcontinental trains – the railroad equivalents of Route 66, if you will.

The California Zephyr runs 2,447 miles between Chicago, Illinois and San Francisco, California. It takes 51 hours 20 minutes to cross the seven states and three time zones involved. Highlights include crossing the Rockies between Denver, Colorado and Salt Lake City, Utah, and traversing the snow-capped Sierra Nevada between Reno, Nevada and San Francisco.

The Texas Eagle is even longer, running 2,728 miles for 65 hours 20 minutes from Chicago to Los Angeles, via St. Louis, Missouri and the Texan cities of Dallas, Austin and San Antonio.

The railcars on both routes are double-decker steel Superliners and the upstairs lounge cars offer magnificent views of the many mountains, canyons, rivers, lakes, prairies, salt flats, deserts and big skies that are yours to behold for the length of the journey. If you travel on either of these train services, you will have seen more of the USA in under three days than most Americans see of their own country in their lifetime.

BELMOND HIRAM BINGHAM (MACHU PICCHU, PERU)

The luxury train service that covers the journey from Cusco to the lost city of the Incas at Machu Picchu is named after Hiram Bingham, the American explorer who rediscovered the ruins in 1911. The blue-and-gold train is impressive; the views of

Peruvian villages and llama herds are quite splendid; and the on-board Peruvian meals are a treat (think Maras beef with root confit, Quillabamba peanuts and a tartar of white grape and myrtle, or Wayllabamba trout with fava beans, Andean mint and airampo cactus emulsion), especially when washed down with pisco sours. It is still difficult to argue, though, that this rail service is all about the journey, not when the destination is at or near the top of most people's bucket lists.

One surprising thing for many people about the rail journey, though, is that it is downhill. Although Machu Picchu is 2,430 metres above sea level, the starting point at Cusco is considerably higher, at 3,400 metres. Hence the train needs to descend into the Sacred Valley of the Andean foothills before following the Urubamba River to Aguas Calientes (Hot Springs), from where you need to climb by bus, or on foot, 390 metres back up again to Machu Picchu itself.

Note: The Belmond Hiram Bingham is pretty expensive for a railway journey of just 3 hours 30 minutes. If your budget doesn't stretch to around £900 for the round trip, then you can travel for a fraction of that price on Peru Rail or Inca Rail. The views will be the same en route and you will still get to see Machu Picchu when you get there.

CONQUERING
THE LANDSCAPE

*There is nothing like a train
journey for reflection.*
TAHIR SHAH

Linked to the main railway lines designed to transport passengers from one town or city to another, many of the world's urban sprawls depend on their own metropolitan networks to the extent that they would soon come to a shuddering halt without them. Away from towns and cities, many unique systems have branched away from main lines into more remote corners to meet the specific needs of the communities they serve.

Metropolitan systems tend to run beneath, above or alongside clogged-up road networks, while community railways are more likely to have been built to link towns and villages across difficult terrain, or to generate much-needed income from the world's tourists. Let us first look beneath the surface.

UNDERGROUND RAILWAYS

As we have seen, London led the way in 1863 when it decided to go underground with a rail network that survives to this day. Budapest followed suit in 1896 and many others have been added around the world since, to the extent that there are now getting on for 200 underground systems in over 50 different countries. Here are some facts and figures about just a few of the underground train systems that now run wholly or partially below the surface of Planet Earth:

- ▶ The **New York City Subway** in the USA has the most stations (468) and lines (24) of any underground system. It provides a 24-hour service on every single day of the year, which is entirely appropriate for The City That Never Sleeps. It was at least partially inspired by the Great Blizzard of 1888 and it remains the best way to travel around the city in freezing winter conditions.

- ▶ The **Beijing Subway** in China opened in 1969 and enjoyed a major extension leading up to the 2008 Beijing Olympics. It now carries the most passengers of any subway system in the world, with up to 13 million jumping on each day (it gets quite crowded).

- ▶ The **Seoul Metropolitan Subway** in South Korea is one of the cleanest, most efficient and most technically advanced passenger services in the world, having digital multimedia broadcasting, high-speed 4G, Wi-Fi and wireless broadband on every station and train. It is also one of the world's largest underground networks, and is therefore a rare combination of virtual and physical superhighway. The subway really got itself noticed in 2012 when it suddenly appeared on screens around the world, twice. Firstly, a subway train and station in the Gangnam District appeared in pop star Psy's 'Gangnam Style' video, the one with the horse dance that went viral worldwide. Secondly, several of its stations appeared as filming locations in the Hollywood blockbuster *The Bourne Legacy*.

▶ There are four lines on the **Budapest Metro,** but Line 1 is the most famous. It was the first underground railway line to be built on the European mainland (in 1896), and the entire line was designated a UNESCO World Heritage Site in 2002.

▶ The longest escalators in an underground station anywhere in the world are at the Park Pobedy Station on the **Moscow Metro**. They are 127 metres long, have 740 'steps' and take almost 3 minutes to reach the surface or platforms. As Moscow underground stations are widely regarded as the most beautiful in the world, this isn't really a problem. Just enjoy.

▶ There are some fine examples remaining of the *fin-de-siècle* art nouveau style adopted at station entrances to the **Paris Métro** in France around the turn of the nineteenth century, including those to be found at Châtelet, Abesses and Porte Dauphine.

▶ The shortest underground railway in the world is the **Minatomirai Line** in Yokohama, Japan. It has six stations and runs for just 2.5 miles to link Yokohama Station, one of the busiest mainline stations in the world, with Yokohama Chinatown.

▶ The **Glasgow Subway** in Scotland is one of the world's shortest, with just 15 stations arranged in a circle. There are two tunnels, so that several trains can travel simultaneously in either a clockwise or anticlockwise direction. The livery of the trains was bright orange for over three decades, giving it the nickname 'Clockwork Orange'. The subway is the third oldest in the world, after London and Budapest, and the only underground line in the UK to be wholly underground.

GREAT RAILWAY ACHIEVEMENTS

Mail rail

The London Tube is well known around the world, but not so many people knew about the narrow-gauge, driverless, underground Post Office Railway that came into service in the city in 1927 to avoid the congestion of the streets above. At its peak, the miniature railway carried over 20 million letters and packages a day at speeds of 30 miles per hour between sorting offices. It ran below Oxford Street, extending for a total of 6.5 miles between Paddington to the west and Mount Pleasant sorting office in the Clerkenwell area to the east. It operated until 2003, when the growth of email finally put paid to the need for it. In 2017, an exhibition about the railway was opened in the new Postal Museum in Farringdon, which includes a 20-minute ride on the miniature trains.

RAILWAYS IN THE SKY

Some cities have preferred to look up to ease their congestion. This has been great news for tourists in particular, because these sky-high systems offer a low-cost bird's-eye view of some of the world's greatest cities while transporting us to and from airports, hotels, sporting venues and attractions. Just like underground systems, they also provide a wonderful insight into the daily life of these cities, because we get to share the space with locals travelling to and from their workplaces, shops and schools. Here are just a few examples of the aerial pleasures available to us today:

- ► It is worth travelling on the driverless, elevated **Docklands Light Railway (DLR)** in London just to see the magnificently regenerated Docklands area. The visual treats for passengers include the River Thames, the O2 arena (Millennium Dome) and Canary Wharf. Opened in 1987, the DLR has since been extended to several lines, including the one out to Stratford International which was built to support the London 2012 London Olympics. A low point came in 1996 when the IRA planted a bomb under a bridge at South Quay station, killing two people and injuring many others. (I was in an office overlooking the station at the time, but fortunately for me the government building I worked in had bomb-proof windows.)

- ► If ever a city needed an air-conditioned, sky-high transport system, it was Bangkok. Stay luxuriously cool in the **Bangkok Skytrain** while pitying the hot, seething mass of humanity below as it mixes with the exhaust fumes of gridlocked traffic. It is an exotic experience to travel with Bangkokians, and temple-spotting from the air passes the time nicely if you do get bored mingling with the locals. Opened in 1999, its wonderful official title is the 'Elevated Train in Commemoration of HM the King's 6th Cycle Birthday'.

▶ Originally experienced only at the world's theme parks and airports, elevated **urban monorail systems** now also abound in cities around the world, including Dubai, Kuala Lumpur, Las Vegas, Mumbai, Moscow, São Paolo, Singapore and Tokyo. Even the world's fastest trains, the maglevs, now run along monorails, even if they don't quite touch them – they don't magnetically levitate more than a few centimetres from them either, though.

▶ The Hängebahn (hanging railway) systems on Dortmund University campus and at Düsseldorf airport are driverless, suspended railways. If you think an **H-bahn**, as they are also called, is a terribly modern idea, you're wrong (see below).

TRAIN OF THOUGHT
'WE ARE PLEASED TO ANNOUNCE THAT ALL SERVICES HAVE BEEN SUSPENDED UNTIL FURTHER NOTICE'

The world's first monorail system, the Wuppertal Suspension Railway (*Wuppertaler Schwebebahn*) is also one of the most unusual metropolitan systems in the world, having transported passengers in its hanging carriages above the German city of Wuppertal since 1901. It takes 30 minutes to travel along underneath the monorail for the entire 8.3-mile journey.

In 1950, a circus decided to transport a baby elephant along the line as a publicity stunt, but the poor animal became frightened and crashed out of the carriage into the River Wupper 12 metres below. Miraculously, it sustained only minor injuries and the train operator and circus director got off with fines.

FUNICULAR RAILWAYS

Funicular railways tend to have two counterbalancing trains navigating a steep slope while attached to the same cable. In very simple terms, this means that the force of the down train helps to pull the other train up, following which the 'up train' repays the favour on the way back down. The first modern funicular railway designed to get citizens up and down a steep slope opened in Lyon, France in 1862. Budapest, on the Buda side going up to the castle, followed in 1870 (although it did have to be rebuilt after being bombed to bits during World War Two). The idea soon caught on and many of the world's steepest hills were soon being conquered by funicular, including the following worthy examples:

▶ The world's steepest cable-driven funicular railway is the **Katoomba Scenic Railway** in the Blue Mountains of New South Wales in Australia. The 52-degree incline achieves a vertical lift of 310 metres and is perfect for acclimatising you for what comes next, which is hanging over the gorge 270 metres below on the Scenic Skyway cable car.

▶ The **Peak Tram** funicular railway carries passengers almost a mile up to the higher reaches of Hong Kong Island, 368 metres above the harbour below. It had three classes when it opened for general service in 1890: first class was for British colonial figures and Victoria Peak residents; second class was for British military and Hong Kong police; and third class was for all other humans and animals. They all got the same view back down over Victoria Harbour, Lamma Island and the business district. I liked it so much that the photo I had taken up there remained my Facebook profile pic for years afterwards.

► The English seaside resort of Bournemouth has three funiculars to carry passengers between the beach and the clifftop town, including the world's smallest, the **Fisherman's Walk Cliff Lift**, which is only 39 metres long. One of the others, the East Cliff Lift, remains closed at the time of writing following a landslide in 2016.

► **Montmartre Funicular** in Paris has been taking grateful tourists up to the basilica of Sacré-Cœur and the artist colony at Place du Tertre since 1900. The alternative is 300 steps, but many people find those easier on the way down. Unusually, each of the two trains has its own counterweight, as opposed to relying on each other for counterbalance, which means at peak times they can both keep climbing as quickly as they can unload and load their own passengers (and keep operating independently if the other one breaks down).

► The **Wellington Cable Car** in New Zealand is a funicular popular with tourists, but it also serves to get local commuters to work and students to university. There are also around three hundred private mini-funiculars in the hilly city to get residents and their shopping home.

► The **Cairngorm Mountain Railway** funicular in the Scottish Highlands is the longest (1.22 miles) and highest (1,097 metres) funicular railway in Britain. The panoramic view from the top is breathtaking and, on the day I was there, included a rainbow 200 metres below and a rare opportunity to see some mountain-dwelling ptarmigans.

► There are three **Lisbon funiculars** to transport locals and tourists alike up and down the steep slopes of the

Portuguese capital: the Lavra, the Gloria and the Bica. The Lavra was the world's first street funicular when it opened in 1884, and it continues to conquer the 25 per cent gradient of the Largo da Anunciada today. All three funiculars are amongst the world's most photogenic, resplendent in their iconic canary-yellow livery. They are also the world's most intimate funiculars; as they carry you up and down the narrow, winding streets, sometimes just inches from the doors and windows of the tall buildings they rub shoulders with, you can see inside houses and even smell family dinners being cooked.

TRAIN OF THOUGHT
'FUNICULÌ, FUNICULÀ'

Having failed to learn the lessons of AD 79, the Neapolitan authorities gave permission in the late nineteenth century for the construction of a funicular railway to the top of Mount Vesuvius. Surprisingly, the man awarded the contract to build the railway was Thomas Cook, the English Baptist minister responsible for the birth of the package holiday 40 years earlier, and so not exactly renowned as a builder of funicular railways! But build it he did, and the famous Neapolitan song 'Funiculì, funiculà' (meaning 'funicular up, funicular down') was composed in 1880 to celebrate its opening.

Destroyed three times in the twentieth century following eruptions of the volcano it was attached to, they finally gave up on the railway following the third of those eruptions in 1944. However, talk of rebuilding the line has sprung up again in recent years. When questioned about the safety of such a proposal, a spokesman for the regional transport authority was quoted as saying, 'If it erupts, it erupts.' Having never been one to let molten lava put me off my next train journey, I'm definitely up for it.

TRAMWAYS

Tramways are the world's 'street railways'. The biggest difference between conventional railways and tramways is that tramways have grooved rails sunk into the streets they share with other modes of transport. In this way, they don't interfere with the progress of the cars, buses and lorries that need to cross over the rails, although cyclists do need to be careful not to get their wheels stuck in the grooves.

The world's first tramway was the Welsh Swansea and Mumbles Railway, which opened in 1807. In common with many of the early tramways, it started as a horse-drawn service before progressing to steam-driven mechanical trams in the late nineteenth century and then switching to overhead electricity in the twentieth century. It finally closed in 1960.

Today, most of the world's tramways remain powered by overhead electric cables via trolley poles or pantographs attached to the roof of a tramcar, although the cable cars of San Francisco remain a significant exception. Let's have a look at some of the most famous tramways, many of which are still running today.

Streetcars and cable cars

The Americans preferred to call their trams 'streetcars' or 'trolley cars'.

▶ The first streetcar line opened in New York City in 1832, followed by **New Orleans** in 1835. The five operating streetcar lines in New Orleans today include the St Charles Streetcar Line, the oldest continuously operating street railway system in the world. The Desire Line that ran through the French Quarter to Desire Street between 1920 and 1948 is the one that is immortalised in Tennessee Williams' 1947 play *A Streetcar Named Desire*.

▶ The first successful cable-operated street railway in the world opened in **San Francisco** in 1873. A further 22 lines were opened by 1890 and the system became a template for others around the world. A steel grip fitted to the underside of the cable car clawed itself around the steel cables that ran below, allowing the car to be hauled up steep inclines and to have its speed controlled on the equally steep declines. The electric-powered tramways of the twentieth century soon replaced the world's cable-car systems, largely because the latter were costlier to maintain, but the cable car survived in San Francisco because it remains more suited to the city's dangerously steep hills. Three lines continue to operate there today, and it is one of the best travel experiences anywhere to stand outside on the running board holding onto a pole as you climb or descend the steep hills enjoying views that include San Francisco Bay and Alcatraz.

Double-deckers

Only three public tramway systems around the world continue to operate double-decker trams: Hong Kong, Alexandria and Blackpool.

▶ **Hong Kong** has the largest double-decker fleet anywhere, with over 160 brightly coloured trams that carry more than 200,000 passengers a day. If you ever find yourself in Hong Kong when there is horseracing on, you can even catch a tram out to Happy Valley, the best-named racecourse on the planet.

▶ The **Alexandria Tramway** in Egypt opened in 1863 and still has 20 lines covering 20 miles of track. It is the oldest tramway system running in Africa. Trams with curtains cost twice as much to ride as those without and the special 'tram cafe' started up in 2015 costs five times more again (but that's still only about 50 pence).

▶ The **Blackpool Tramway** runs for 11 miles along the Fylde Coast between Blackpool and Fleetwood. One of the oldest electric tramways in the world, it carries over five million passengers a year on its heritage double-decker 'balloon cars' and ultramodern single-deckers.

World-leading Melbourne
Melbourne has the largest tramway network anywhere in the world, with 160 miles of track, 24 routes, nearly 500 trams and 1,763 tram stops. I particularly recommend Route 96 to St Kilda, not only because it is considered to be one of the finest tram rides in the world, but also because it delivers you straight to Melbourne's happening beachfront playground. Three of Melbourne's vintage W Class trams have even been converted to provide the Colonial Tramcar Restaurant service around the city, with one lunch and two dinner sittings each day.

The next largest of the world's tramway systems are St Petersburg (127 miles), Upper Silesia in southern Poland (124 miles), Berlin (118 miles), Moscow (112 miles) and Vienna (107 miles).

MOUNTAIN RAILWAYS
We have already looked at some mountain railways in the Great Train Journeys chapter, which is not surprising because mountain railways are by their very nature wonderfully scenic. They are also monuments to the men who built them,

who somehow managed to triumph over nature in its most inhospitable form. More often than not, as we have seen, they were built with narrow-gauge track, which is more suited to the twists and turns necessary to negotiate mountainsides. A general rule of thumb is 'big mountain, small railway'. Here are some more climbing railways that will literally take your breath away when you get to the top, and leave you wondering whether there is anything that human beings cannot achieve when they put their minds to it:

- ► In 1865, the **Ffestiniog Railway**, the world's first steam-driven, narrow-gauge railway, started carrying quarry slate and passengers between the town of Blaenau Ffestiniog, 230 metres above sea level, and the harbour in Porthmadog below. This magnificent line in north Wales is operational today as a restored heritage railway and offers wonderful views of Snowdonia.

- ► The **Harz Narrow Gauge Railways** in northern Germany form a good, old-fashioned, proper railway system. Across a narrow-gauge network of 87 miles straddling the old border between east and west, its huge locomotives include 1950s 2-10-2T steam locomotives working their 14 wheels off to get up and over the mountain range day after day, year after year, in all weathers; its diesel railbuses (yes, they do look like a cross between a train and a bus) are equally impressive. For tourists and rail enthusiasts alike, it is a wonderful step back in time to the golden age of steam, vintage diesel and sheer muscle power. For the citizens of the many mountain towns and villages connected by the network, though, it remains their lifeline. It gets them to work and to the shops, and it gets their children to school.

► The electric **Snaefell Mountain Railway** on the self-governing Isle of Man is the only surviving operational Fell railway system in the world (at least it was until it was shut down in late 2017 as a result of health and safety checks following a brake failure, so make sure you check that it has reopened before turning up). On a clear day, the views from the top of Snaefell, the highest point on the island, are said to stretch across six kingdoms: the Isle of Man, England, (Northern) Ireland, Scotland, Wales and Heaven.

Fell railway systems, named after their English designer John Barraclough Fell and not because they climb fells (which they do), employed a raised third rail between the outer rails for extra traction and braking, and were once used in France, Italy, Brazil and New Zealand. They were largely replaced by rack-and-pinion or cog railways, which gripped trains to the rails more effectively than Fell systems ever could.

► The **Mountain Railways of India** have been designated a UNESCO World Heritage Site on account of the profound impact they had on social and economic development in the late nineteenth/early twentieth century; because they served as models for many others around the world; and because they remain living operational examples of engineering genius. The three railways that comprise the 'site' are the Darjeeling Himalayan Railway in the north-east of the Himalayas (see the Great Train Journeys chapter), the Kalka–Shimla Railway in the north-west of the Himalayas, and the Nilgiri Mountain Railway in the southern state of Tamil Nadu. In other words, they are nowhere near each other, but all three offer stunning views of their respective terrains.

► One of the main problems with the Klondike Gold Rush of the 1890s was the need to get equipment-laden mules to and from the US port of Skagway (at the top of Alaska's Inside Passage) over the White Pass of the Coast Range Mountains. The **White Pass and Yukon Route Railroad** from Skagway to Whitehorse in Canada's Yukon Territory would ultimately provide the answer, but only after the gold rush had come and gone in 1900. As luck would have it, copper, silver and lead were found in greater abundance than gold and the railroad was in business. It eventually closed in 1982, but since then parts of it have been restored to provide vintage mountain-railway excursions to the 800,000 cruise-ship passengers who turn up in Skagway each year.

TRAIN OF THOUGHT
THE TALE OF 'SOAPY' SMITH

As if it wasn't difficult enough to build the White Pass and Yukon Route Railroad over the high, rugged territory between Alaska and the Yukon Territory (450 tons of explosives and quite a few pick-axe-wielding navvies were needed), 'Soapy' Smith made it even harder. The Old West crime-gang boss tried everything to sabotage the railway, the completion of which would prevent him from extorting tolls from mule-driving prospectors as they crossed over the mountain. A vigilante gang was set up to deal with the problem and 'Soapy' met his end in a shootout in 1898. The railroad resumed blasting after helping to capture the rest of the gang by blocking off their escape routes.

TRAIN FERRIES

Train ferries are so called because they have railway tracks that allow carriages on a through service to roll onto a boat at one harbour and roll back off again at a different harbour on the other side of the body of water in question. Their heyday may have come and gone, many such services having been replaced by increasingly sophisticated rail bridges and tunnels, but they are still more common than you might think. Here are just a few of the past and present train ferries which capture the imagination:

▶ In 1850, the *Leviathan*, the world's first modern train ferry, started to operate on a roll-on/roll-off basis across the **Firth of Forth** in Scotland, between Granton and Burntisland. Known as the 'Floating Railway', it ran until replaced by the Forth Bridge in 1890.

▶ In the second half of the twentieth century, British Rail went as far as buying and operating their own ferries to get their rolling stock across the **English Channel** to France, with the intention of getting passengers from London to Paris overnight without the need for them to leave their sleeping compartments. The last such night ferry ran in 1980, by which time cheaper airfares had rendered the business uncompetitive.

▶ The biggest roll-on/roll-off train ferry in the world is the MV *Skåne*, built in 1998 to carry freight trains (and trucks) across the **Baltic Sea** between Trelleborg in southern Sweden and Rostock in northern Germany. Its eight railway tracks, including two that are lowered to a different deck once they are laden with railway carriages, cover a total distance of 0.68 miles. You can also cross the Baltic Sea as a passenger on the high-speed Hamburg–

Copenhagen line, while your train has a well-earned rest between Germany and Denmark on the Puttgarden–Rødby ferry.

Other train ferries that continue to transport freight and/or passenger trains include those that cross the following waterways of the world:

- ▶ **Messina Strait:** carries passenger and freight trains between Calabria in the toe of Italy and Messina on Sicily.

- ▶ **Caspian Sea:** there are several train ferries across this stretch of water, linking the railways of Azerbaijan with those of Turkmenistan.

- ▶ **Gulf of Alaska and northern Pacific Ocean:** tugboats pull train barges between Alaska and the contiguous USA at Seattle. This is a long way to tug a train but the alternative of building a railroad the length of the Coast Range Mountains (largely through Canada) doesn't bear thinking about.

- ▶ **Cook Strait:** the Interislander service ferries trains 50 miles back and forth between Wellington on the North Island and Picton on the South Island of New Zealand.

- ▶ **Qiongzhou Strait:** carries trains between mainland China and Hainan Island. These are very choppy waters, so getting the boat tracks lined up horizontal with those on the harbour is no mean achievement.

- ▶ **Yangtze River:** the Jianying Train Ferry carries freight trains across the river 24 times in both directions daily.

STARS OF SCREEN

*There was no doubt in my mind that steam
engines all had definite personalities.*

REVEREND W. AWDRY

As all film buffs know, one of the earliest moving films seen by a cinema audience was of a train coming into the Gare de La Ciotat in the south of France. The 50-second film was shot by the Lumière brothers in 1895 just after they had invented the movie camera. There is an apocryphal tale that some members of the audience ducked down behind the seats in fear of their lives as the train drew closer to the screen.

Trains have continued to appear on screen ever since, in countless films and TV programmes around the world. They starred in many of the silent movies of the early twentieth century, and directors of the 'talkies' have found it equally difficult to resist the lure of train romances, hold-ups, hijacks and fights, especially fights that take place on the roof of a moving train as the inevitable tunnel looms ever larger at head height in the background. James Bond, Indiana Jones, the Lone Ranger, Zorro, Wolverine and Spider-Man are but a few of the action heroes who have had to survive 'Look-behind-you' moments while grappling with their arch enemies at rock-and-roll speed.

There are too many train-related screenings to cover in anything less than the size of a small library, so here are just some of the best to allow you to relive some long-forgotten viewing pleasures, or perhaps prompt you to go and catch some others that you may have missed:

SILENT MOVIE TRAINS

In 1903, the first movie ever to tell a story was the 12-minute-long *The Great Train Robbery*, a classic (silent) Western in which four bandits hold up a train with no violence spared.

The early twentieth century seemed to be a time in history when there was a constant need for heroes to untie damsels in distress from railway tracks seconds before they would have been cut in three by thundering steam locomotives. This led to the mistaken belief in Hollywood that 'standard gauge' on railroads was set at the average distance between the neck and ankles of a standard-issue damsel in distress.

One of the earliest (and best) full-length films to star trains on the big screen was *The General*, a 1926 silent movie based on a real American Civil War incident. Full of dangerous train stunts, it starred co-director Buster Keaton as Johnnie Gray, a Confederate railway engineer. After Union soldiers hijack a Confederate train (an American-type 4-4-0 locomotive), Johnnie gives chase in another 4-4-0, the *Texas*, initially unaware that his true love, Annabelle Lee (Marion Mack), is held captive on the stolen train ahead. In the best traditions of Hollywood, he eventually foils the pesky Yankees and recovers Annabelle. In the most expensive stunt of the silent-movie era, however, one of the locomotives does not have such a happy ending, being allowed to collapse into the river below as it crosses a sabotaged bridge in Cottage Grove, Oregon. After filming, the locomotive was left in its wrecked state in the riverbed as a minor tourist attraction for almost 20 years, until it was broken up for scrap during World War Two.

ALFRED HITCHCOCK AND THE RAILWAYS

In 1935, Alfred Hitchcock was the first of three directors in the twentieth century to make a film based on John Buchan's 1915 novel *The Thirty-Nine Steps*. He cast Robert Donat as Richard Hannay, the man on the run (more often than not, by train) from eve-of-war Prussian spies. London St Pancras and Edinburgh Waverley are just two of the stations where Hannay has narrow escapes from his pursuers, and another hair-raising moment centres on his escape from the train on the iconic Forth Bridge near Edinburgh. One of the steam locomotives to star in the film was an A3 Class Pacific (think *Flying Scotsman*).

Hitchcock would return to the railways again and again for his film settings, most notably in *The Lady Vanishes* (1938), *Strangers on a Train* (1951) and *North by Northwest* (1959).

SPOTTING TRAINS IN DAVID LEAN FILMS

David Lean got straight to it when it came to including railways in his films, going so far as to set his fourth film, *Brief Encounter* (1945), wholly within a railway station.

The classic film tells the story of a married (but not to each other) middle-aged couple (played by Trevor Howard and Celia Johnson), who fall in love following a chance meeting at Milford Junction, which was in fact Carnforth Station in Lancashire, at that time a junction of the London, Midland and Scottish Railway. One of the reasons Lean chose Carnforth as a filming location was that it was far enough away from the blackout zones that encircled the cities of wartime Britain at the time.

The couple converge on the station from opposite directions on a weekly basis, and such is the film's enduring popularity that the waiting room where much of their doomed love affair unfolds has been restored in recent years to look as it did at the time of shooting. You can still travel by train to the Heritage Centre at the station and have a cup of tea or something to eat in the same refreshment room used in the film.

Like Hitchcock, train enthusiast Lean was also drawn time and again to the railways, not least for the setting of *The Bridge on the River Kwai* (1957) and for many of the scenes in *Lawrence of Arabia* (1962) and *Doctor Zhivago* (1965).

THE RAILWAY CHILDREN (1970)

Based on Edith Nesbit's 1906 book of the same name, this 1970 classic children's film remains cult viewing for adults yearning for the age of innocence, steam and a cracking good yarn. Starring Dinah Sheridan, Bernard Cribbins and, as the children, Jenny Agutter, Sally Thomsett and Gary Warren, it centres on the desire of the Waterbury children to clear the name of their father, wrongly imprisoned as a spy. The children plan and plot in between waving to the trains that go by on the line near their home. As well as managing to clear their father's name with the help of an old gentleman commuter and the local station porter (Bernard Cribbins), they also find time to avert a rail crash by warning an approaching train of a landslide (achieved through the waving of the girls' red petticoats); reunite a Russian dissident with his family; and care for the old gentleman commuter's grandson after he breaks a leg in a paper-chase accident.

There is no doubting the authenticity of the railway setting or the trains used in the film. It is set on the preserved Keighley and Worth Valley Railway in Yorkshire, including the station at Oakworth, and the steam locomotives used included a

Lancashire and Yorkshire Railway Class 25 engine and a Nigel Gresley-designed Great Northern Railway Class N2 side-tank engine (which remains operational today on the Middleton Railway in West Yorkshire).

The same, alas, cannot be said for the authenticity of the 'children'. Sally Thomsett was cast as 11-year-old Phyllis but was in fact aged 20 at the time, while the 17-year-old Jenny Agutter played her 20-year-old big sister 'Bobbie'. Thomsett was not allowed to smoke, drink alcohol, see her boyfriend or drive her sports car anywhere near the set.

MURDER ON THE ORIENT EXPRESS

The 1934 Agatha Christie murder mystery has inspired a number of films, plays and TV programmes around the world. Here we look at the two main films to have hit the silver screen.

1974 film

The stars who wanted to spend time filming on board the Orient Express lined up thick and fast for director Sidney Lumet. They included Albert Finney (as Belgian sleuth Hercule Poirot), Richard Widmark, Lauren Bacall, Ingrid Bergman (who won an Oscar for her role), Sean Connery, John Gielgud, Vanessa Redgrave, Michael York, Jacqueline Bisset and Anthony Perkins. You get a better class of actor on the Orient Express.

The plot involves the need for Poirot to resolve the murder of an American ex-Mafia boss (Richard Widmark) on board the Istanbul to London service. The victim is stabbed 12 times in the Balkans (and, let's be honest, there are few worse places to be stabbed in) while the train is stuck in a snowstorm. The absence of footsteps in the snow leads the cunning Poirot to deduce that the murderer or murderers remain on board. (Spoiler alert!

In the film's denouement in the deluxe Pullman dining car, Poirot reveals that all 12 stabbers remained on board!)

Filming locations included the Gare de l'Est in Paris and, for running shots of the train and the snowbound murder scene, the Jura Mountains of the Alps. The steam locomotive used was a stalwart of the French railway system for 50 years, a 230 Class 4-6-0, known colloquially as the Ten Wheel. This particular Ten Wheel, number 230 G 353, is said to have starred in a total of 35 films, so it must have known what was expected of it.

2017 film

The 2017 version directed by Kenneth Branagh has an equally stellar cast, which includes Branagh himself (as Poirot), Judi Dench, Penélope Cruz, Johnny Depp, Willem Dafoe, Derek Jacobi, Michelle Pfeiffer, Daisy Ridley and Olivia Colman.

Neither the train nor its locations are real this time round, however, because the 22-ton working locomotive with tender and four complete carriages (each weighing 25 tons) were in fact built on site at Longcross Studios in Surrey, as was the mile-long track that the train chugs up and down during filming.

TV TRAINS

On television, there has been an explosion of railway-based programmes in recent years, and the BBC in particular can't seem to get enough of them. The *Great British Railway Journeys* and *Great Continental Railway Journeys* programmes presented by Michael Portillo have already recreated hundreds of journeys that originally took place in Victorian Britain and dozens of Continental ones that took place in Europe just before the beginning of World War One.

Trains and railways have also featured heavily in fictional TV series, including the three I have picked out below: the classic mini-series *Love on a Branch Line*, the acclaimed period drama *Downton Abbey*, and the American TV blockbuster *Hell on Wheels*.

Love on a Branch Line (BBC, 1994)

This television adaptation of John Hadfield's eponymous 1959 novel tells the delightful story of Jasper Pye, a refined civil servant sent to rural England to close down a less-than-useful statistical outpost run by three members of staff in the huge stately home that had been commandeered from Lord Flamborough during the Battle of Britain and subsequently forgotten about. Lord Flamborough, who lost both his legs in a train accident while working as an inexperienced driver during the 1929 General Strike, has long since taken up residence in a two-carriage train on a nearby private branch line. Jasper soon loses sight of his mission, falling instead for the idyllic countryside, as well as all three of Lord Flamborough's daughters.

Filming actually took place on the North Norfolk Railway, a heritage steam railway popularly known as the Poppy Line, and at Weybourne Station in particular, which had already starred as fictitious Walmington-on-Sea Station in the 1970s BBC sitcom *Dad's Army* and as equally fictitious Crimpton-on-Sea Station in the 1980s BBC sitcom *Hi-de-Hi!* The two carriages used by Lord Flamborough were third-class electric Pullman carriages that belonged to Southern Railway's 1930s art deco Brighton Belle service, many of whose carriages are currently being restored to their former glory for mainline use.

Downton Abbey (ITV, 2010–15)

This classic British period drama is renowned as much for its attention to historical detail as it is for its storylines and high quality of acting. It is not, therefore, surprising to learn that Downton Station is in fact the beautifully tended Horsted Keynes

Station on the steam heritage Bluebell Railway in Sussex. If you want to travel in the post-Edwardian splendour enjoyed by Lord and Lady Grantham and the rest of the Crawley family, book a trip on the Bluebell Railway when they are running their first-class Pullman carriages. But do sit up straight!

Hell on Wheels (AMC, 2011–16)

This multi-award-winning Western TV series depicted the building of the Transcontinental Railroad across America in the 1860s and largely followed the trials and tribulations of the Union Pacific Railroad as it crossed the Great Plains. Conditions were so tough for the labourers, surveyors, mercenaries, preachers, bartenders and prostitutes who lived and often died in the mobile encampment as it moved west that the encampment gained the nickname 'Hell on Wheels'. This TV production brilliantly captures the harshness and dangers they faced and proved so popular that it ran for five series.

In 2016, ITV had a decent stab at a similar programme in Britain, called *Jericho*, which was set in a shanty town in the Yorkshire Dales at the time the Ribblehead Viaduct was being built in the 1870s. It was dubbed Britain's 'first TV Western', but it didn't prove popular enough to warrant a second series.

BOLLYWOOD ON RAILS

The Indian film industry, known as Bollywood, has enjoyed a long and successful relationship with Indian Railways, with countless love scenes and action sequences shot in, on and around trains. One 7-minute sequence shot for the 1998 movie *Dil Se..* ('With Love') stands out above the rest. It features Shah Rukh Khan (known to his millions of fans as SRK) and a large cast in a song and dance routine on top of a moving train as it snakes its way through the Nilgiri Mountain Railway in

Tamil Nadu. They gyrate to A. R. Rahman's chart-topping hit 'Chaiyya Chaiyya', seemingly untroubled with the health and safety aspects of giving it your all on top of a moving train. It isn't just one of the great Bollywood moments; it is one of the great moments in cinematic history.

The Darjeeling Limited was another great film set on Indian Railways, but it was made by Hollywood, not Bollywood (see below).

The Darjeeling Limited (2007)

This beautifully filmed madcap adventure about three brothers (played by Owen Wilson, Adrien Brody and Jason Schwartzman) travelling across India on a train is based on a misguided attempt by one of the brothers to get the three of them to bond with each other and at the same time achieve some spiritual enlightenment. The train sequences were filmed on the North Western Railway line that runs through the Thar Desert between the stunning Rajasthani cities of Jodhpur and Jaisalmer. Director Wes Anderson borrowed a diesel locomotive and ten carriages from the railway company there and then revamped the carriages according to a design that was partially inspired by the interiors of the 20th Century Limited service that ran between New York and Chicago until 1967.

HOGWARTS EXPRESS

As all Harry Potter fans know, the Hogwarts Express leaves London King's Cross Platform 9¾ for Hogsmeade Station without fail at 11 a.m. on 1 September each year, and thereafter at the beginning of each term. Harry first meets Ron Weasley and Hermione Granger on the train and the trio go on to enjoy many a chocolate frog served by 'the trolley witch' during their long journeys together.

Towards the end of their journey the train is filmed passing along the real-life West Highland Line from Fort William to Mallaig (opposite the Isle of Skye), with the beautiful Glenfinnan Viaduct featuring prominently in many of the shots. The *Hogwarts Castle* locomotive, originally built by the Muggles at Crewe to run on steam but now powered entirely by magic, is in fact the Great Western Railway Hall Class 5972 *Olton Hall*, now based at the National Railway Museum at Shildon in County Durham. Your only chance as a Muggle to ride the Hogwarts Express is to hop on board the impressive replica that now runs between Universal Studios and Universal's Islands of Adventure in Florida.

TRANSSIBERIAN (2008)

Many films have been purportedly set to some extent or another on the legendary Trans-Siberian Express, including the epic *Doctor Zhivago*. In the case of Brad Anderson's 2008 film *Transsiberian*, the entire plot, which is a mix of murder, deception and drug-running, centres around the seven-day diesel-powered train journey from Beijing to Moscow. Woody Harrelson, Ben Kingsley and Emily Mortimer try their level best to outshine the iconic train and the Siberian scenery, but it's a tall order. An American couple, Roy (Woody Harrelson) and Jessie (Emily Mortimer), take the Trans-Siberian Express for the initial stage of their journey home from China, because Roy is a train enthusiast and can't resist the lure of one of the longest railway journeys in the world. The excitement reaches levels even Roy could not have foreseen, though, when he has to take control of the locomotive himself in order to make good the couple's escape from villainous Russians. If only someone had told him that there was another train coming from the opposite direction along the same track…

FILMED AT GRAND CENTRAL TERMINAL

The many great Hollywood movies to have been filmed to one extent or another at Grand Central Terminal in New York include thriller *North by Northwest* (1959); crime drama *Carlito's Way* (1993); sci-fi action comedy *Men in Black* (1997); tragic drama *Revolutionary Road* (2008); train-based thriller *The Taking of Pelham 123* (2009); mystery thriller *The Girl on the Train* (2016); and superhero film *Spider-Man: Homecoming* (2017). However, the only one to be centred solely within the vicinity of the station is *The Taking of Pelham 123*.

The Taking of Pelham 123 (2009)

This film is a remake of a 1974 film based on Morton Freedgood's book of the same name. The tense plot is centred on the armed hijacking of the 1.23 p.m. New York Subway train out of Pelham Bay Park, and a subsequent ransom demand in exchange for the lives of the passengers and train conductor who have been taken hostage. John Travolta plays the chief hostage-taker, while Denzel Washington had the critics drooling over his performance as the subway company employee on the other end of the difficult negotiations.

One of the main differences between the 1974 version (which starred Walter Matthau and Robert Shaw) and this one is that the earlier film was shot within Grand Central Terminal, while this one was filmed on carriages deep within the subway tunnels. This drive for claustrophobic authenticity came at a price, though, as director Tony Scott, along with John Travolta, Denzel Washington and others working on the movie, had to take the NYC Transit Authority's 8-hour training course that is a prerequisite for anyone intending to walk on the rail tracks. Judge for yourself if the added authenticity was worth it. (It was.)

SNOWPIERCER (2013)

Based on a French graphic novel of the same name, this South Korean sci-fi thriller directed by Bong Joon-ho and enjoying a star-studded Hollywood cast (including Chris Evans, Jamie Bell, Ed Harris, Tilda Swinton and John Hurt) brings train films into the future. It is set after a failed climate-change experiment kills everyone on the planet except those who were lucky enough to have boarded the *Snowpiercer*, a massive train that hurtles non-stop around the globe behind a perpetual-motion engine, over and over again. A class system and a divided economy are quickly established, and life on board the train becomes a microcosm of how the world was before disaster struck – until, 17 years on, the lower classes at the back of the train decide that enough is enough. The revolution (pun intended) is underway.

TRAINS IN WESTERNS

I doubt if anyone has ever counted the number of Westerns featuring trains over the years, but I'm pretty sure the answer is 'a lot'. Many of the ones that spring to our minds are old classics like *The Iron Horse* (1924) and *Jesse James* (1939), but mostly they're from the golden age of Westerns in the 1960s and 1970s. Great films like *How the West Was Won* (1962), *Once Upon a Time in the West* (1968), *Butch Cassidy and the Sundance Kid* (1969), *The Train Robbers* (1973) and *Breakheart Pass* (1975) wouldn't be quite the same without their train scenes.

However good they were, though, none have done it better than the more recent *The Lone Ranger* (2013), starring Armie Hammer as the Lone Ranger and Johnny Depp as Tonto. I'm pretty sure that train scenes in Westerns don't get much better than The Lone Ranger riding Silver along the top of a moving train with guns blazing in all directions. Displaying a fine sense of history, the producers even included a scene that depicted the Golden Spike Ceremony that took place when the Transcontinental Railroad came together at Promontory Summit in Utah in 1869.

A huge oval track in the middle of nowhere in New Mexico (but still close enough to Albuquerque not to get entirely lost) was just one of five railroad locations purpose-built for the many train scenes in *The Lone Ranger* by the magnificently named Gandy Dancer Railroad and Excavating Services. Two diesel locomotives, a 4-6-0 Ten-Wheeler and a 4-4-0 American, were both built from scratch and could both reach speeds of up to 40 miles per hour, which was in fact the speed of the originals in their day.

After filming, the trains were donated to the Fillmore and Western (F&W) Railway in California, which is known as the 'Home of the Hollywood Movie Trains', because most of its stock has been acquired from 20th Century Fox, Paramount, Warner Bros. and MGM over the years. The F&W has been used in more than 400 movies, TV series and commercials, but it still manages to run a year-round tourist train. If you turn up there, there's a decent chance you might just see some filming.

THE 15:17 TO PARIS (2018)

This Clint Eastwood film is based on the actual events of 21 August 2015, when three young American friends (Anthony Sadler, Alek Skarlatos and Spencer Stone) were travelling together on a Thalys train service that had left Amsterdam at 15.17 for Paris. After a terrorist emerged from the toilet in their carriage armed with a range of weapons, including an AK-47 rifle, a pistol, a knife and enough ammunition to kill a lot of the passengers on board, and with little regard for their own safety, they tackled and eventually disarmed the gunman.

Stone, an off-duty airman, kept a grip around the terrorist's neck in spite of being slashed several times by the terrorist's knife. Once Skarlatos, an off-duty member of the National Guard, had beaten the terrorist unconscious, Stone then saved the life of a French passenger who had been shot in the neck by sticking two fingers into his wound to stem the loss of blood from an artery. All three friends, plus three Frenchmen and a Briton who also stood up to the gunman, were later awarded the *Légion d'honneur* in recognition of their bravery. Unusually for a Hollywood movie, Clint Eastwood cast the three young Americans as themselves, in spite of the fact that none of them had any previous acting experience.

Note: Thalys is a multinational high-speed train company owned and operated by the French, Belgian and German national railways.

CAPTURING
THE MAGIC

I never travel without my diary.
One should always have something
sensational to read in the train.
FROM OSCAR WILDE'S *THE IMPORTANCE*
***OF BEING EARNEST* (1895)**

Trains made a huge and immediate impact on the world when they burst into public consciousness, so it is not surprising that painters, lyricists, musicians, writers and poets soon sought to capture the essence and romance of rail travel in their works. In this chapter, we will look at some of their most significant offerings.

AN ARTIST'S IMPRESSION

Trains were an exciting new subject for artists in the nineteenth century, presenting them with opportunities to depict the raw power of steam, capture motion within landscape and portray human reactions to the possibilities of travel. They certainly made an impression on the French impressionists, many of whom took lodgings or a studio close to the Gare Saint-Lazare in Paris.

Claude Monet was so fascinated by the golden age of steam trains that he painted the subject 11 times. In 1998 the Musée d'Orsay in Paris and the National Gallery of Art in Washington DC even put on an exhibition entitled *Manet, Monet and the Gare Saint-Lazare*.

But it wasn't just the impressionists who were impressed. Here are some of the best-known railway masterpieces to grace our gallery walls:

Artist: J. M. W. Turner
Painting: *Rain, Steam, and Speed – The Great Western Railway* (1844)
Current location: National Gallery, London
A typically atmospheric depiction by the English Romantic landscape painter of a Gooch Great Western 4-2-2 steam locomotive racing across the Maidenhead Railway Bridge between London Paddington and Reading just six years after the line had opened. The intensity of light and colour soon had Monet and others studying Turner's technique.

Artist: Augustus Egg
Painting: *The Travelling Companions* (1862)
Current location: Birmingham Museum and Art Gallery, West Midlands
Egg uses a train compartment as a Hogarth-style setting to depict the differences between two almost identically dressed Victorian ladies sitting opposite one another. One is perfectly prim and proper, industriously reading her book with her gloves on, a basket of flowers at her side; the other displays signs of not adhering entirely to the Victorian values of the day, having given in to idleness by falling asleep, her hands gloveless and thereby exposed for all the world to see, and with a basket of (forbidden) fruit at her side. The train is travelling alongside the

Mediterranean in the south of France, an area to which many Victorians, including Egg, travelled by train in the hope of improving their health.

Artist: William Powell Frith
Painting: *The Railway Station* (1862)
Current location: Royal Holloway University of London, Egham, Surrey
This huge canvas by the English social painter contains over a hundred characters at Paddington Station in London. The cast-iron and glass structure of the station and the steam locomotive would have appeared ultramodern at the time, and Frith makes a point of displaying the vast amounts of luggage that Victorians travelled with when they took to the rails.

TRAIN OF THOUGHT
THE MAN'S NOT EVEN DEAD!

When William Powell Frith's huge canvas of London Paddington was first unveiled in 1862, *The Times* reported that he had been paid the staggering sum of £8,750 for it, going on to point out that such amounts had traditionally been reserved for the works of dead painters.

Artist: Camille Pissarro
Painting: *Lordship Lane Station, Dulwich* (1871)
Current location: Courtauld Institute of Art, London
A small, soot-blackened steam locomotive, viewed from a footbridge, takes centre stage as it puffs towards us out of what was then still a rural station on the Crystal Palace and South

London Junction Railway. What the Danish-French impressionist painter depicted was the modernity of a changing world, because the suburban housing depicted in the background was then mushrooming at the same pace as an ever-growing rail network.

Artist: Édouard Manet
Painting: *Le Chemin de Fer (The Railway)* (1873)
Current location: National Gallery of Art, Washington DC
The French impressionist Manet was one of those who took rooms near the Gare Saint-Lazare, the biggest and busiest station in Paris at the time. In fact, the doors to his studio are visible across the other side of the Gare Saint-Lazare in this painting. A young girl clings to the railings as she gazes down at a steam locomotive on the tracks below, while the woman beside her sits with her back to the railings, perhaps having seen it all before.

Artist: Claude Monet
Painting: *Arrival of the Normandy Train, Gare Saint-Lazare* (1877)
Current location: Art Institute of Chicago, Illinois
Fellow French impressionist Monet takes us right inside the Gare Saint-Lazare, but still manages to convey the impression of a landscape scene, with smoke from the trains taking on the role of clouds. He had to work quickly to capture the moment of light, steam and motion as trains arrived at the station, and the canvas, now in Chicago, is just one of seven that he painted of the station within three months to exhibit at the third impressionist exhibition in Paris.

TRAIN OF THOUGHT
WHEN IS A RAILWAY STATION NOT A RAILWAY STATION?

The Gare d'Orsay in Paris, built in the Beaux Arts style in 1900 but rendered largely redundant by 1939 on account of its short platforms, reopened in 1986 as a stunning art museum, the Musée d'Orsay. It houses the largest collection of impressionist and post-impressionist masterpieces in the world, including works by Monet, Manet, van Gogh, Gauguin and Renoir. One of the finest views in Paris today is looking out from the top level of the museum through one of the former station's two giant clocks, across the Seine to Sacré-Cœur in the north of the city.

Artist: Vincent van Gogh
Painting: *Le Train Bleu* (*The Blue Train*) (1888)
Current location: Musée Rodin, Paris
One of four van Gogh paintings that included a train, this is the view that the post-impressionist Dutch artist captured of a long, blue freight train as it crossed over the viaduct near Arles, as seen through the trees in a park. Arles is the town in the south of France where he stayed in 1888 in the 'yellow house', his painting of which also included a steam train in the background.

Artist: Edward Hopper
Painting: *House by the Railroad* (1925)
Current location: Museum of Modern Art, New York City
Given his propensity for straight, clean lines, Hopper was always going to be able to make good use of railroad tracks, streamlined locomotives and railroad carriages. And he did just that, again and again. This particular painting, the very first to be acquired

by the Museum of Modern Art in 1930, captured the isolation and loneliness of a railroad track in the middle of nowhere in between trains, with only an abandoned American Gothic mansion for company. It portrays the clash between the faded grandeur of a bygone rural way of life and the exciting world of modernisation brought about by the American railroad system – a struggle which, it seemed, could only have one winner.

Artist: Terence Cuneo
Painting: *Night Freight (Condor)* (1960)
Current location: Private collection
English artist Terence Cuneo was an accomplished painter of many subjects and possibly most famous for being the official artist at the coronation of Queen Elizabeth II. He is known in railway circles for his depictions of trains, many of which have appeared on countless book jackets, catalogues, jigsaws, railway advertising posters and postage stamps. His originals can be seen in many British museums, galleries and other institutions, and a bronze statue of him by renowned Scottish sculptor Philip Jackson stands at London Waterloo Station as a memorial to his contribution to railway art.

The painting I have chosen to highlight here is the one he did of the 'Condor' night freight service that ran between London and Glasgow in the 1950s and 1960s, because I think it captures perfectly the immense power of a British Rail Class 28 diesel locomotive in full flow. The Class 28 was never in fact the most reliable of locomotives, but you wouldn't think so to look at Cuneo's depiction of it.

THE POSTER ART OF NORMAN WILKINSON
English artist Norman Wilkinson was first and foremost a marine painter, who also put his skills to patriotic use when he designed

the 'dazzle camouflage' that protected merchant ships from torpedoes during World War One. One of his marine paintings (*Plymouth Harbour*) hung in the first-class smoking room of the *Titanic* but is probably not in the best condition by now.

He is also known to millions for the advertising posters that he designed and drew for the London and North Western Railway and the London Midland and Scottish Railway in the early twentieth century, enticing British and foreign tourists alike to come and sample the delights of the British Isles by train. He made everywhere look positively idyllic, and he must have been responsible for countless numbers of rail holidays that would not otherwise have happened. In his posters, Colwyn Bay became the 'Gateway to the Welsh Rockies'; Belfast Lough was the 'Gateway to Happy Holidays'; Devon was the area to go to 'For Sunshine and Sea Breezes'; and the Scottish Highlands and Islands promised 'Holidays on Land and Sea'.

TRAIN OF THOUGHT
RAILWAY BATHING BEAUTIES

A London, Midland and Scottish Railway poster produced in 1937 by Italian artist Fortunino Matania highlighted the charms of Southport Lido in Merseyside by displaying a slightly risqué (for its time) sketch of female bathing beauties. A copy of the poster was sold at auction in 2006 for just under £8,000, having been bought two weeks earlier for £14. That must have caused a titter or two at the back of the room.

MUSICAL TRAINS

Trains are by their very nature rhythmic, so perhaps it was inevitable that they would find their way into every conceivable form of music, from classical to jazz and boogie-woogie, from blues and country to rock and pop. Here are some examples to illustrate the widespread appeal of the sound and romance of trains:

Tune: *Pacific 231* (1923)
Style: orchestral
Recorded by: Arthur Honegger
The *mouvement symphonique* that propelled Swiss composer and train enthusiast Honegger to fame depicts the sound of a Pacific 231 steam locomotive, a class of locomotive that is more commonly known as a 4-6-2 (in many European countries the conventional notation counts axles rather than wheels, hence 2-3-1). The piece was later used as the soundtrack to a short film of the same name in 1949, a film that so vividly captured the majesty of the steam locomotive that it won the Short Film Palme d'Or at Cannes that year.

Tune: 'Chattanooga Choo Choo' (1941)
Style: big-band swing
Recorded by: Glenn Miller and His Orchestra
After featuring in the 1941 musical film *Sun Valley Serenade*, this Oscar-nominated record was the first ever to receive a gold disc (1.2 million sold) and remained at number one for nine weeks. It was written while the composers Harry Warren (music) and Mack Gordon (words) were travelling on the Southern Railway's 'Birmingham Special' between New York City and Birmingham, Alabama via Chattanooga, Tennessee. The train they had in mind was not the one they were travelling on, though, as their inspiration apparently came from a 2-6-0

Mogul wood-burning steam locomotive they had seen en route on that same railroad.

The iconic song has since been covered by many of the established stars of the music business, including Cab Calloway, Carmen Miranda, Bill Haley & His Comets, Elvis Presley, The Shadows and Barry Manilow.

Tune: 'The Loco-Motion' (1962)
Style: pop
Recorded by: Little Eva
The song that everybody liked to line-dance to while pretending to be a train was written by Carole King and Gerry Goffin and performed by Eva Boyd, the bubbly teenager who used to babysit for them. As Little Eva, the babysitter took the song to number one in the USA and number two in Britain. The appropriately named Grand Funk Railroad, an American blues rock band, took it back to the top of the US charts with an alternative version in 1974, and Australian 'pocket rocket' Kylie Minogue had worldwide success in 1988 when she gave the song the Little Eva treatment all over again.

Tune: 'Last Train to Clarksville' (1966)
Style: pop/rock
Recorded by: The Monkees
The catchy debut single of the fun-loving quartet, who were soon to become America's answer to the Beatles. In the year that followed, in fact, they outsold The Beatles and The Rolling Stones put together. The lyrics constitute a plea from a young man about to be drafted into the Vietnam War that his sweetheart should hop on the last train to Clarksville, so that they might spend some final moments together before he goes off to war. Clarksville was close to the US Air Force base in Tennessee from which many troops were sent overseas.

Tune: 'Hear My Train A Comin'" (1967)
Style: blues rock
Recorded by: Jimi Hendrix
Said to have been written by Hendrix to evoke the longing for the arrival of the all-important train that would take cotton pickers north to a better life after the American Civil War. He often performed the song live and it was also considered important enough to be one of the 12 tracks included in the 1973 'rockumentary' about the singer's life.

Tune: 'Casey Jones' (1970)
Style: rock
Recorded by: Grateful Dead
An update by the eclectic US band of the traditional folk song 'The Ballad of Casey Jones' on their 1970 *Workingman's Dead* album. The original ballad, most famously covered by American country legend Johnny Cash, and the Grateful Dead version both referred to the true story of engine driver Casey Jones, who died in 1900 while trying to stop his collision-bound 4-6-0 Ten-Wheeler, the *Cannonball Express*. He slowed the train enough to save the lives of all passengers on board, but not his own, and a railroad legend was born. He later became immortalised not just in music, but also on film and in TV programmes bearing his name.

Tune: 'Midnight Train to Georgia' (1973)
Style: soul
Recorded by: Gladys Knight & the Pips
The song that even people who can't sing like to sing, this soulful classic became the band's Grammy-winning signature tune. If you'd rather live with him in his world than be without him in yours, you should know by now when the next train leaves for Georgia.

Tune: 'Slow Train' (1979)
Style: gospel rock
Recorded by: Bob Dylan
This was a song on the *Slow Train Coming* album that Dylan wrote to declare himself a born-again Christian. It sounded as Dylan as Dylan ever was, and it benefited from having Mark Knopfler of Dire Straits fame on lead guitar. The pen-and-ink album cover pays homage to the navvies who built the American railroads.

Tune: 'Crazy Train' (1980)
Style: heavy metal
Recorded by: Ozzy Osbourne
The very first single from the English legend's very first solo album (*Blizzard of Ozz*) begins with the words 'All aboard!' and has as its chorus, 'I'm going off the rails on a crazy train.' The guitar solo on the track is often voted one of the best of all time, so Randy Rhoads, Ozzy's lead guitarist, must have been inspired by the rhythm of the train in his mind while he composed it.

Tune: 'Train Medley' (1980)
Style: country hobo
Recorded by: Boxcar Willie
One of many train compositions performed by the appropriately named country music singer, who sang in 'old-time hobo' style. Given that his albums included *Daddy Was a Railroad Man* and *King of the Freight Train*, and that he listed his instruments as 'guitar' and 'train whistle', most people knew of his passion for US railroads and trains. Not so many people knew that he was a US fighter pilot during the Korean War.

Tune: *Musique à Grande Vitesse* (High-speed Music) (1993)
Style: classical (for orchestra and ballet)

Recorded by: Michael Nyman Band and the National Orchestra of Lille
Written by English composer Nyman to commemorate the opening of the new Paris–Lille TGV (*train à grande vitesse*) line in 1993. When you listen to this piece, you won't be able to imagine yourself anywhere other than on a high-speed train racing through the French countryside.

Tune: 'Slow Train' (2011)
Style: blues rock
Recorded by: Joe Bonamassa
The prolific US singer/songwriter/guitarist is one of many artists who have helped to bring the train song bang up to date in the twenty-first century (others include John Mayer, Kelly Clarkson, Josh Turner and AC/DC). This offering is from his 2011 *Dust Bowl* album, so don't expect trains to disappear from song lyrics any time soon.

TAKING TRAINS LITERALLY

Writers and poets have been just as keen as artists and musicians to jump on board the bandwagon. Many writers, such as Agatha Christie, used trains as the setting for some of their most famous stories. Others, like Leo Tolstoy and Boris Pasternak, used them as thematic imagery throughout their epic tales (*Anna Karenina*; *Doctor Zhivago*). P. G. Wodehouse even used them for comic effect, when he had Roderick Spode, the 'amateur dictator' of the Jeeves and Wooster books, announce the widening of the gauge of the entire British railway network 'so that sheep might stand sideways on trains'.

Authors of children's books have also made impressive use of trains to get their messages across, including, of course, the Reverend W. Awdry, whose bestselling stories from The Railway

Series have made worldwide icons of Thomas the Tank Engine and his friends. Another children's author to personify trains to great effect was Arnold Munk, whose 1920 story of *The Little Engine That Could* inspired generations of children to give of their best in the knowledge that they could succeed if they only tried hard enough.

Here are just a few examples of train-related literature that has educated, entertained and inspired generations of readers:

Charles Dickens' ghost train

Dickens' short story 'The Signal-Man' (1866) centres around the signalman's visions of a ghost waving and shouting at him from the mouth of a nearby railway tunnel, and the fact that a rail tragedy of some kind or other inevitably occurs following each vision. Dickens wrote the story shortly after narrowly surviving a fatal rail accident himself. He had been on board when the London to Folkestone boat train derailed over a viaduct in June 1865, killing 10 and injuring 40 passengers.

Through the Looking-Glass (1871)

In the sequel to *Alice's Adventures in Wonderland*, author Lewis Carroll puts Alice in a crowded railway carriage without a ticket. The guard inspects her through a telescope, a microscope and a pair of opera glasses before deciding that she is travelling in the wrong direction. The other passengers, including a goat, a beetle and a horse, make rude comments about her stupidity, but she soon forgets about all this when the train suddenly flies through the air to cross a brook and deposits Alice under a tree, next to a gnat. You just couldn't make it up!

Tolstoy and trains

Near the beginning of Leo Tolstoy's 1877 novel *Anna Karenina*, a railway worker accidentally slips under a train in

Anna's presence, which she considers to be a very bad omen. She's not wrong. The omen continues to haunt her as she is torn apart by her ill-fated love affair and doomed marriage. Trains appear throughout the novel in line with some of the more dramatic twists and turns of the plot, and at the end a desperate Anna commits suicide by throwing herself under a passing train, turning the earlier omen into a self-fulfilling prophecy.

Ironically, Tolstoy himself died in a Russian railway station (Astapovo) in 1910 after taking a train to escape his own troubled marriage. He contracted pneumonia on the train and the stationmaster offered him his bed on which to recuperate – it would soon become his deathbed. He didn't get to die in peace over the course of the week he spent at the station, because the world's press had been able to get there quickly and easily on a kind of macabre railway special straight to the spot. In one of the earliest-known examples of frenzied media intrusion, newspaper reporters wired daily updates about nothing very much to their various home countries, and were joined by a Pathé News camera team eager to catch any final glimpses to be had of the great man. They were all rewarded with a scoop when he did indeed pass away at the station.

La Bête humaine (1890)

This psychological thriller by the French novelist Émile Zola was set on the Paris–Le Havre railway line and involved a train driver and a deputy stationmaster and his wife in murder, lust and infidelity. A train derailment, a rail suicide and a runaway train at the outbreak of the Franco-Prussian War all help to keep the action hurtling along the tracks, and evocative descriptions of engine drivers battling to control their steaming locomotive beasts add bucketloads of atmosphere.

Keeping track of Sir Arthur Conan Doyle

Of Arthur Conan Doyle's 60 Sherlock Holmes stories, 44 involved rail travel. This is not too surprising, given that in Victorian Britain the only travel alternative was a horse-drawn coach or a rudimentary bicycle. However elementary the solution might turn out to be, one simply cannot solve complex mysteries quickly while bouncing up and down rutted tracks on very little suspension, so the train was the only reasonable means of transport to get the job done.

In one other story, 'The Lost Special' (1898), he does not mention his 'amateur reasoner of some celebrity' by name, but it is clearly Sherlock himself who investigates the disappearance of a privately hired train between Liverpool and London. The only people on board were the engineer, the fireman, a guard and two South Americans, but it turns out that the Italian mafia are behind the disappearance.

George Bradshaw in literature

His fame may have been resurrected in recent years by the BBC series *Great British Railway Journeys* and *Great Continental Railway Journeys*, presented by former British cabinet minister Michael Portillo, but George Bradshaw was even more famous during the period his railway timetables and associated travel guides were actually in print (between 1839 and 1961).

His guidebooks were referred to countless times in popular literature, including Jules Verne's *Around the World in Eighty Days* (Phileas Fogg sets off with his Bradshaw to conquer the world's circumference), and Bram Stoker's *Dracula* (the eponymous count refers to a Bradshaw's guide to plan how to get himself and his coffin from Whitby to London). Other popular writers to refer to a Bradshaw's guide include Charles Dickens, Sir Arthur Conan Doyle (there was always a copy of Bradshaw's at 221b Baker Street), Agatha Christie and Lewis Carroll, but perhaps Bradshaw's crowning literary glory is that a copy of his own 1863 railway guide was included in a time capsule under Cleopatra's Needle on London's Victoria Embankment in 1878, along with a set of British coins, a portrait of Queen Victoria, the Bible, and photographs of 12 of the best-looking English ladies of the day!

Agatha Christie's train mysteries

Everyone is aware of Agatha Christie's fictional Belgian detective Hercule Poirot and his ability to solve the most complex of crimes, even while travelling on a train.

In *The Mystery of the Blue Train* (1928), Poirot is intent on minding his own business when he boards *Le Train Bleu* in Paris, bound for the French Riviera. (But we all know better, don't we, boys and girls?) One strangled American heiress, one missing ruby and one murderous male impersonator later, Poirot does what Poirot does best: solving complicated murders while minding his own business.

Christie's Belgian detective, of course, most famously solves the murder of an American passenger in the 1934 mystery *Murder on the Orient Express*, a book so popular it has spawned countless TV, film and theatre versions, a trend that continues to this day.

But it's not just Poirot that Agatha Christie employed to solve train mysteries. In 1957, she also had the elderly English spinster and amateur detective Miss Jane Marple solve a train murder in her *4.50 from Paddington* novel, a book that was turned into the 1961 film *Murder, She Said*.

Strangers on a Train (1950)

This was American author Patricia Highsmith's first novel, a psychological thriller in which two strangers meet on a train and discuss the possibility of swapping murders so that neither will have a motive in the eyes of the police. Charles Anthony

Bruno, a psychopathic playboy, wants his father murdered, whereas Guy Haines, an architect, would quite like his wife out of the way so that he can take up with his mistress. Haines doesn't take Bruno's suggestion to swap murders too seriously, but he has to think again after Bruno murders his wife. Haines eventually returns the favour, but he lacks the nerve to live with his guilt and ultimately confesses all after Bruno has accidentally drowned.

Master of suspense Alfred Hitchcock turned the book into a film the year after its publication.

Fast-tracking 007

Ian Fleming often involved British secret agent James Bond in train-related danger in his books, and in the 1957 novel *From Russia, With Love*, he has his spy playing out much of the action on board the Orient Express. Copious amounts of intrigue, passion, personal combat, shootings and murder keep up the pace in the Pullman dining car and in the suite that Bond has booked for himself and the defecting Soviet beauty Tatiana Romanova. Bond makes a rare mistake when he is fooled into thinking that his would-be nemesis, a Russian executioner whose homicidal tendencies coincide with the full moon, is a fellow MI6 agent. That error occurs in the dining car when Bond glosses over the Russian's giveaway culinary faux pas when the latter orders red wine to go with his fish.

Jim Stringer novels

A series of detective novels by contemporary English writer Andrew Martin has railwayman Jim Stringer reassigned to the London and Southwest Railway police in Edwardian England, where he solves a number of crimes before spreading his wings to do the same thing in further-flung places, including Iraq and India. You know that you are in for train-related literary treats just by looking at the book titles, which include: *The Necropolis Railway*, *Murder at Deviation Junction*, *Death on a Branch Line*, *The Baghdad Railway Club* and *Night Train to Jamalpur*.

The Railway Series

A total of 42 books revolving around Thomas the Tank Engine were written in The Railway Series between 1945 and 2011, initially by rail enthusiast and cleric the Reverend W. Awdry himself, and later by his son Christopher. At first glance, they are brilliantly simple children's stories about personified trains on the fictional Island of Sodor. On closer inspection, they are based on actual British railway lines and locomotives, and on real-life events such as the closure of branch lines throughout the UK in the 1960s and the replacement of steam by diesel. Illustrators have come and gone, as have narrators of the spin-off television series, but the popularity of the stories and characters is undiminished to this day.

It is also the case that many famous locomotives have made 'guest appearances' in The Railway Series. In book number 35, *Thomas and the Great Railway Show*, for example, Thomas gets invited to visit the National Railway Museum in York, where he can barely conceal his excitement at meeting *Rocket*, *Iron Duke*, *Mallard*, *Duchess of Hamilton* and *Green Arrow*.

The real-life Thomas and friends

If you have ever wondered which 'real-life' trains the Reverend W. Awdry chose as his models for The Railway Series, here are just a few to get you started:

Fictional character	Actual locomotive	Service history
Thomas the Tank Engine	Billinton 0-6-0T (tank) E2 Class steam locomotive	Shunting and short-haul freight services on the London, Brighton and South Coast Railway
Gordon the Big Engine	Gresley Pacific 4-6-2 A3 Class steam tender engine	Mainline passenger services on the London and North Eastern Railway
Henry the Green Engine	Stanier Class 5 4-6-0 steam tender engine	Utility locomotive on the London, Midland and Scottish Railway, known as the 'Black Five'
James the Red Engine	Class 28 0-6-0 steam tender engine	Passenger and freight services on the Lancashire and Yorkshire Railway
Bill and Ben	W. G. Bagnall 0-4-0ST (saddle tank) steam locomotives *Alfred* and *Judy*	Purpose-built for industrial service around tight curves and under low bridges in and around Par Harbour in Cornwall
Daisy	Class 101 DMU (diesel multiple unit)	The lightweight DMU that started to replace steam locomotives on UK branch lines in the 1960s
Pip and Emma	British Rail Class 43 InterCity 125 high-speed diesel	The high-speed train that still holds the world speed record for diesel trains

Poetical trains

Given that poetry and trains have rhythm in common, this was another inevitable union. In fact, such was the allure of the steam age in Britain that *Night Mail*, a 1936 documentary about the overnight London to Glasgow Postal Special, included a poem written by poet W. H. Auden and set to music by composer Benjamin Britten. The poem is recited to the rhythmic beat of the *Scots Guardsman* steam locomotive thundering down towards the Scottish border as the mail is being sorted in the carriages behind. Here are some other examples of riveting railway-related rhymes you might come across in the many poetry anthologies that exist to evoke the spirit of the railway:

Poem: 'From a Railway Carriage' (1885)
Poet: Robert Louis Stevenson
The Scottish novelist and poet included this poem in his collection *A Child's Garden of Verses*, in which he describes trains as 'faster than fairies' and 'faster than witches'. Stevenson was also a travel writer and by the age of 28 he had crossed the USA by train from New York to California (although his primary reason for doing so was to resume a love affair with an older American woman, whom he later married). He wrote about his transcontinental railroad journey in a travel memoir called *Across the Plains* (1892).

Poem: 'On the Departure Platform' (*c.*1910)
Poet: Thomas Hardy
The sweet sorrow of parting is perfectly encapsulated following a farewell kiss at a station ticket barrier, becoming increasingly poignant as the man left behind can only stand back and watch his sweetheart getting smaller and smaller as she walks down the 'diminishing platform'.

Poem: 'Adlestrop' (1917)
Poet: Edward Thomas
A wonderful description of a moment in time, captured when the poet was on a train that made an unscheduled stop on a hot summer's day in 1914 at the tiny village of Adlestrop in Gloucestershire. 'No one left and no one came' on account of the express train having stopped there 'unwontedly'.

Poem: 'Harrow-on-the-Hill' (1954)
Poet: John Betjeman
The English Poet Laureate was a great rail enthusiast who used the images and sounds of trains, railways and stations in a number of his poems. This one appeared in a collection called *A Few Late Chrysanthemums* and refers to the electric trains that are lit up 'after tea' in the melancholy of autumn. As we have seen, Betjeman was the saviour of St Pancras Station in the 1960s, and in 1973 he presented a TV documentary called *Metro-Land* about the growth of the Metropolitan Railway across north-west London in the early twentieth century.

Poem: 'The Whitsun Weddings' (1964)
Poet: Philip Larkin
The train poem to end all train poems. The English master of verse captures perfectly the many weddings he witnesses from his train seat as he travels one sunny Saturday afternoon from Kingston-upon-Hull (where he worked as a librarian) to London. He doesn't just spot weddings, though, he spots 'short-shadowed cattle', 'acres of dismantled cars', an Odeon cinema that 'went past' and a cricketer running up to bowl. Travelling in the days when train windows could be opened properly, he is also able to capture the smells of early summer in the countryside and towns that he passes through.

Poem: 'The Railway Children' (1972)
Poet: Seamus Heaney
From his *Wintering Out* collection, this short poem is one of Heaney's many beautiful evocations of his childhood in Northern Ireland.

THEATRICAL TRAINS

You might think that trains are not a natural fit for the theatre, but some playwrights and theatre impresarios beg to differ:

The Ghost Train (performed 1925–27)

Written by Arnold Ridley, the English actor and playwright who went on to play Private Godfrey in the British sitcom *Dad's Army*, this play was a mystery thriller involving train passengers who had become stranded overnight at a disused railway station and then advised not to clap eyes on the ghost train that would pass through for fear of the inevitable death that would follow. The ever-popular Ghost Train rides at British fairgrounds are said to have taken their name from the play, which was also later produced as a book and adapted for the cinema three times.

The very next year saw the first production of *The Wrecker*, another of Ridley's plays with a train theme, this time concerning an old engine driver whose locomotive had become a bit too self-important. The production of both plays involved train appearances that required elaborate special effects for their day.

Starlight Express (performed from 1984 onwards)

It is said that the English musical impresario Andrew Lloyd Webber originally wanted to base a musical on Thomas the Tank Engine and Ridley's friends in The Railway Series books, but that the Reverend W. Awdry wasn't prepared to give him the amount of poetic licence he wanted. Instead, his rock musical

Starlight Express is based on toy trains racing around inside the dreams of a small boy, with the trains portrayed on stage by roller-skating actors. Steam, diesel and electric locomotives try to outdo one another to win the all-important race, with *Rusty*, the ageing steam locomotive, prevailing against all the odds. The Starlight Express did in fact exist as a service on British railways in the late 1950s and early 1960s, running during the night at weekends between London and Glasgow.

Starlight Express was one of the longest-running musicals in London's West End, from 1984 until 2002, and has toured worldwide. It has been running in Germany since 1988 and remains one of the biggest shows in that country.

The Railway Children (performed 2005–17)
This is Mike Kenny's Olivier Award-winning stage adaptation of the 1906 Edith Nesbit book that also enjoyed great success as a film of the same name in 1970. The show enjoyed runs at the British National Railway Museum in York, Waterloo and King's Cross stations in London, and Toronto's Heritage Railway Museum in Canada. Purpose-built theatres surrounded a real rail track, and the show featured some of the biggest guest stars ever to tread the boards: one of a number of original steam locomotives on loan from the British National Railway Museum.

The 39 Steps (performed from 2005 onwards)
Picking up on a 1995 small-scale comic adaptation by Simon Corbie and Nobby Dimon in North Yorkshire, Patrick Barlow re-adapted it in 2005 for the West Yorkshire Playhouse before hitting the big time in London's West End. It is the theatre production of the 1915 John Buchan novel, which has, of course, already enjoyed success as a film on three separate occasions. This time it is played for laughs, with only four actors playing 130 characters for 1 hour 40 minutes, which is achieved through

the mechanism of quick-fire costume and accent changes. This becomes particularly frantic during the on-board train scenes, when comic timing to the rhythm of the train becomes everything.

KEEPING THE
DREAM ALIVE

*It means more to me to be on the
cover of* Model Railroader *than to
be on the cover of a music magazine.*
ROD STEWART

A lot of people spend a lot of time and effort preserving, modelling, travelling on, playing with or just enthusing about trains and railways. Many of them got the bug working on the railways for real; many have never shaken off the thrill of the first train set they received from Father Christmas; and many have needed a serious hobby to spend their cash on or fill their spare time with. They all have one thing in common: a love of trains and railways. This chapter is dedicated to those who preserve trains and railways that would otherwise be lost forever, those who painstakingly reproduce the real thing in miniature model form, those who collect railway memorabilia, and those who spend anything up to an entire lifetime spotting and recording whatever moves on two rails.

HERITAGE RAILWAYS

Railways generally need preserving by private groups when a government or national railway company has deemed them no longer profitable or worth funding, or after they have fallen into disrepair following the end of their useful working life. The vast majority of them become heritage railways, which is to say that they enjoy a new lease of life as a tourist attraction. Railway preservation is a costly business, no matter how many volunteers step forward to give up their time for the cause, so the income from tourism is vital to the survival of most preserved railways.

Such is the determination and enthusiasm of the people who do step forward to preserve this important part of their cultural history that there are now thousands of heritage railways dotted around more than 40 of the world's countries. Here is a very small sample to alert you to the bewildering array of choices on offer:

Bluebell Railway
Location: East and West Sussex, England
Original parent railway: London, Brighton and South Coast Railway
Type: standard gauge, steam
Length of track: 11 miles

The first preserved standard-gauge, steam-driven passenger service in the world, railways like this one allow us to relive the golden age of steam. A particular highlight is the Golden Arrow Pullman experience, a recreation of the glamorous London to Paris service once favoured by those who liked to fine-dine on the go. The railway has over 30 steam locomotives, around 150 carriages and wagons, and a station (Sheffield Park) that has been restored to its original Victorian splendour. A film-maker's paradise, the railway's star appearances have included some classic British productions, including the 1985 film *A Room with a View*, the acclaimed period drama series *Downton Abbey* and the very final episode of revered sitcom *It Ain't Half Hot Mum*.

Strathspey Steam Railway
Location: Scottish Highlands
Original parent railway: Inverness and Perth Junction Railway
Type: standard gauge, steam and diesel
Length of track: 10 miles

This railway runs from the ski resort of Aviemore through Boat of Garten (famous for its osprey population) to Broomhill (the station known to millions of *Monarch of the Glen* viewers in Britain as 'Glenbogle'). If ospreys aren't your thing, you could watch out instead for the family of oystercatchers (the little waders with the long bright-orange beaks) that nest every spring between the lines of the railway between Broomhill and Boat of Garten.

Although they have plenty of diesel back-up, most of the heritage runs are hauled by a majestic-looking LMS (London, Midland and Scottish Railway) Ivatt Class 2 2-6-0 steam locomotive.

Giant's Causeway and Bushmills Railway
Location: County Antrim, Northern Ireland
Original parent railway: Giant's Causeway, Portrush and Bush Valley Railway
Type: narrow gauge, steam and diesel
Length of track: 2 miles

It might be only 2 miles long, but at one end it has Northern Ireland's top tourist attraction, the Giant's Causeway, and at the other the home of one of the world's favourite tipples, the Bushmills Distillery. In between stations, you can admire sand dunes and a links golf course, both typical of this part of the country. This railway started life as the world's longest electric tramway but is now largely diesel-powered, with the odd 'steam special' being tugged along by one of its two small (0-4-0) tank engines.

THE PLEASURE TRAIN

The longest pleasure pier in the world is at Southend-on-Sea in Essex, reaching 1.34 miles out into the Thames Estuary. That makes the diesel-powered, narrow-gauge Southend Pier Railway the longest pleasure-pier railway in the world, because its sole purpose is to carry passengers from shore to pier head and back again.

California Western Railroad
Location: Mendocino County, California
Original parent railway: Fort Bragg Railroad
Type: steam, diesel, railcars
Length of track: 40 miles

This heritage line provides excursions through redwood forests, crossing some 30 bridges and passing through two deep mountain tunnels. It goes by the nickname of the 'Skunk Train' because you used to be able to smell its gas-powered railcars before you could see them.

Locomotive highlights are the 1924 Baldwin (Mikado) 2-8-2 steam engine and the bright-yellow 1925 Edwards Rail Car Company single-unit motor car (the one that ran on crude oil and gave the 'Skunk Train' its name).

North Borneo Railway
Location: Sabah, Malaysia
Original parent railway: North Borneo Railway
Type: standard gauge, steam
Length of track: 33 miles

Enjoy the sights, sounds and smells of local villages, temples, markets, mangrove swamps, paddy fields, rubber and coffee plantations, lush jungle and the South China Sea, all in a single journey. A British Vulcan 2-6-2 wood-burning steam locomotive pulls beautiful wooden carriages full of passengers doing that most colonial of things: having a piping-hot tiffin lunch served by pith-helmeted, white-uniformed staff while being cooled by the breeze offered by open windows and proper ceiling fans.

Jose Cuervo Express
Location: Guadalajara, Mexico
Original parent railway: Ferrocarriles Nacionales de México
Type: standard gauge, diesel
Length of track: 25 miles

A train that runs full-day excursions through fields of blue agave (the base ingredient of tequila) from Guadalajara to the tequila distillery of Jose Cuervo and on to the town of Tequila itself. Tequila tastings and live mariachi music are provided on board. The scenery is worth seeing, but how much of it you remember rather depends on your tequila intake.

Froissy Dompierre Light Railway
Location: Haute Somme, France
Original parent railway: British and French armies
Type: narrow gauge, steam and diesel
Length of track: 4.3 miles

Also known as Le P'tit Train de la Haute Somme, this railway is the last survivor of the narrow-gauge lines built to supply the British and French armies and their allies serving in the trench-filled battlefields of the Somme during World War One. It has several operational steam and diesel locomotives running alongside the towpath of the River Somme and it houses the Military and Industrial Railways Museum at the Froissy end. The museum displays an impressive collection of 37 vintage locomotives and around a hundred wagons.

Sugar Cane Train
Location: Lahaina, Hawaii
Original parent railway: Lahaina, Kaanapali and Pacific Railroad
Type: narrow gauge, steam
Length of track: 6 miles

As its name suggests, the railway was originally built to haul sugar cane from plantation to mill. The highlight is a 100-metre curved wooden trestle bridge, from which passengers can see neighbouring Hawaiian islands and the volcanic West Maui Mountains. Between December and April each year it is also not uncommon to spot humpback whales in the surrounding waters. The railway has one tender and two saddle-tank steam locomotives, one of which still sports its iconic cowcatcher.

Romney, Hythe and Dymchurch Railway (RH&DR)
Location: Hythe and Dungeness, Kent
Original parent railway: RH&DR
Type: narrow gauge, steam
Length of track: 14 miles

It is clear from the RH&DR that a miniature railway is no small engineering feat! This scaled-down replica of a full-size railway opened in 1926 on a very narrow gauge of 38 centimetres, but was nonetheless built and operated as a public service and continues to provide local school and shopping runs to this day. However, it does now also rely on tourism for its survival.

It is a one-third-scale representation of the London and North East Railway's mainline train service of the 1920s. The locomotives, therefore, include one-third replicas of Sir Nigel Gresley's famous A1 Pacifics. Indeed, Gresley himself was so impressed that he turned up in person at the grand opening in 1926. In another major PR coup, the railway somehow convinced Stan Laurel and Oliver Hardy to come along to the grand reopening in 1947 following World War Two. Stan, at least, had no problem slipping into the scaled-down driver's cab for the publicity shots.

BRANCHING OUT

Not all defunct branch lines have been lucky enough to be restored as operational railways, but some have at least achieved the next best thing following their conversion to walking, cycling and/ or bridle paths. One such success story in England is the Cuckoo Line, a single-track service that once operated in Kent and East Sussex. Even though you can no longer enjoy them from a train, you can still take pleasure in the rural views that once delighted the Cuckoo Line's passengers.

PRESERVATION, PRESERVATION, PRESERVATION

Heritage railways are just one form of railway preservation around the world. Many countries also have one or more railway museums and hundreds of skilled railway engineers continue to restore locomotives and carriages to their former glory so that they can be admired in museums or, even better, travelled on along heritage lines. Whole railway stations have been restored with painstaking attention to detail, from old enamel advertising signs to uniforms that recreate the look of some bygone age or other. From the world's oldest operating steam locomotive to a historically significant luggage van, here is a very brief flavour of what all these preservers are preserving for grateful generations to come.

East India Railways locomotives

The sibling locomotives EIR (East India Railways) 21 and 22 are the world's oldest preserved operating steam locomotives and arrived in India together in 1855. Built by Kitson and Company in Leeds, West Yorkshire, the 2-2-2 tank engines are both running broad-gauge heritage excursions in India today at a top speed of 25 miles per hour.

EIR 21 originally served the East India Company and has just been restored by India's Southern Railway. It is now running steam excursions between Egmore and Kodambakkam in Chennai.

EIR 22, also known as *Fairy Queen*, originally ran mail trains and served as a troop carrier during the Indian Rebellion of 1857. It now runs steam excursions from New Delhi to Alwar in Rajasthan.

Furness Railway No. 20

The oldest preserved operational standard-gauge steam locomotive in Britain, known simply as FR 20, can often be seen at Locomotion, the National Railway Museum site at Shildon in County Durham. It is such a star, though, that it often doesn't get much rest between the guest appearances that it makes across the length and breadth of Britain. A 0-4-0 tender engine, it was originally built in 1863 by Sharp, Stewart and Company in Manchester.

British National Railway Museum

British rail heritage is vast, so vast that its national collection is spread over two sites, the main one being at York in North Yorkshire, the other at Shildon in County Durham. At York alone, there are over 100 locomotives (including *Rocket*, *Mallard* and *Flying Scotsman*) and around 300 other items of rolling stock. It is the most-visited museum in Britain outside of London and it is very difficult not to feel the size and age of a small child as you wander amongst some of the most impressive locomotives ever built. If, like me, you are not unnecessarily tall, many of the locomotive wheels alone will be taller than you are.

There is also a Museum of Scottish Railways at Bo'ness in Scotland and a number of smaller displays attached to heritage railways around the UK, including the Engine Sheds at the Welsh Highland Heritage Railway at Porthmadog.

The 'Mikados' of Japan

Although these Class D51 2-8-2 steam tender locomotives were retired in Japan as long ago as 1975, and only two or three have been restored to operational order, over 170 of them have nonetheless been preserved across the country. Powerful and majestic-looking, these black locomotives (known as *Degoichi* in Japanese) were so revered by Japanese rail enthusiasts that around 8,000 devotees attended a last-rites ceremony when the final ones were retired. (See also 'Brand new steam trains' in the Famous Trains chapter.)

The railroad museums of North America

There are more than 300 railroad museums across the USA and Canada. Only three US states and two Canadian provinces do not have one. Between them, they contain a truly huge number of steam and diesel locomotives and railroad carriages. That's a lot of preservation that's needed right there, one of the reasons that Railcamp is one of the summer-camp options open to American high-school students who might like to take messing around with trains to a serious level.

Passenger luggage van 132

One of the most important preserved railway carriages can be found at the Kent and East Sussex Railway. It was used during its working life for three significant repatriations to the UK.

In 1919, it brought home the remains of Edith Cavell, the nurse who was executed for helping British POWs escape from occupied Belgium, and merchant seaman Captain Charles Fryatt, who was captured and executed after ramming a German U-boat with his ferry while en route from Harwich to the Hook of Holland. When it was decided the following year that the remains of an unknown warrior were to be brought from France to lie amongst the kings and queens buried at

Westminster Abbey, passenger luggage van 132 was again the obvious choice for the job.

CADEBY RECTORY RAILWAY

Men of the cloth have long been drawn to the railways (the most famous example, of course, being the Reverend W. Awdry), and the Reverend Teddy Boston was no exception. He wanted to build a railway in the small garden of his rectory in Cadeby in Leicestershire in the 1960s, but he couldn't afford to buy a scale replica that would fit into it, so he went ahead and bought a real tank engine instead! He purchased a W. G. Bagnall 0-4-0 saddle-tank locomotive from a nearby quarry, which also kindly donated two carriages and 98 metres of track, which was all the track the cleric ever had. The steam train ran up and down the short track until 2005, when it was dismantled and moved to the Moseley Railway Trust in Staffordshire, where it can still be seen.

Fawley Hill Railway

Sir William McAlpine, the same man who rescued *Flying Scotsman* from San Francisco in 1973, didn't have to worry about his garden in Henley-on-Thames not being big enough when he decided to set up a full-size private railway in it in 1964. He has a standard-gauge track of almost a mile in length, which includes the steepest gradient (1:13) of any conventional railway in the world. He has a restored Hudswell Clarke 0-6-0 locomotive, which has to go full pelt to get up the steepest stretch of track (the gradient is the same as the average gradient on the Snowdon Mountain Railway, but with no rack-and-pinion system to grip the locomotive to the track).

Sir William has also amassed a wealth of railway 'artefacts', including several stations, a footbridge, a signal box, two arches from the old Waterloo Station, a two-storey museum full of railway memorabilia, and two carriages that once belonged to Royal Trains. One was formerly the Queen's private carriage; the other was used as a nursery coach for Prince Charles and Princess Anne. Sir William uses them as spare bedrooms for his guests.

Admission to the railway is by invitation only on special open days (it probably helps if you are a group belonging to a club or association involved in railway heritage or preservation).

THE WORLD OF MODEL RAILWAYS

When English inventor Frank Hornby started to produce small-scale clockwork model trains in the 1920s, he could scarcely have envisaged that the Hornby name would be going strong almost a century later or that the world would now have over a hundred model railway manufacturers.

Clockwork has long since given way to state-of-the-art electric power, the latest incarnation of which is digital command control, which allows more than one train to be controlled on the same track at the same time. Manufacturers in different countries produce models to different scales, designed to run on different track gauges.

Size matters

The 00 scale is the standard in Britain, which means that each train model is built to 1/76 the size of the original 'real-life' train and that the track gauge required is a width between the rails of 16.5 millimetres. H0 (1/87) is the slightly different scale used in North America and continental Europe, and was so called because it started life as half the size of the 0 scale that German manufacturers had been building to since the start of the twentieth century. Japan uses the considerably smaller N scale (1/150), which means a lot of trimming for any Bonsai trees they might cultivate as part of the railway's scenery.

Bit by bit

It is needless to say, perhaps, that all other components of a model railway layout need to be built to the same scale as the trains and track. Stations, sheds, bridges, tunnels, railway employees, passengers, cows, sheep and everything else besides are made to an astonishing degree of accuracy with a quite bewildering variety of materials. If you're not a practical person, you can't build a model railway layout from scratch, but you can buy one, bit by bit, and millions of people around the world do just that.

Big business

The model railway business (or railroad modelling business, if you're reading this in North America) is a multibillion-pound industry running alongside a thriving second-hand market, with original pieces from the 1950s and 1960s going for vast sums of money. Clubs and societies span the globe, as do the manufacturers, dealers and magazine publishers required to feed the hunger for all things related to railway modelling.

Miniatur Wunderland

Located in Hamburg, Germany, this model railway consists roughly of 10 miles of H0-scale track, 1,300 trains consisting of 12,000 carriages, 100,000 other moving vehicles, 150,000 trees, 500,000 lights and 400,000 human figurines. If you look very closely, you might even see a small-scale Michael Portillo, which he painted himself when he visited the exhibition during the filming of *Great Continental Railway Journeys* for the BBC. The layout has many different sections, including those set in Hamburg and its airport, the Alps, Austria, Scandinavia, Switzerland and the USA. Planned additions include sections representing Italy, France, England and parts of Africa. The Braun twins, Gerrit and Frederik, and their 270 employees have been building it up since 2000.

CELEBRITY RAILWAY ENTHUSIASTS

If you think that railway enthusiasts generally live at home in the relative obscurity of their loft conversions, away from the outside world and rarely seeing daylight, you might reconsider when you have read the following list of rather well-known celebrities who have found time to indulge in a train-related hobby while doing some other stuff with their lives as well:

- ▶ **Pete Waterman:** as a member of the Stock, Aitken & Waterman hit factory, English record producer Waterman made enough money to indulge his real passion: trains. He pretty much spent his childhood spotting trains on Leamington Spa Station, a complex model of which he has been building at his home for several years. He also owns a number of real, full-size steam and diesel locomotives in various states of repair and renovation, and he even did some work on the *Flying Scotsman* during the time he was part-owner of the train.

- ▶ **Rod Stewart:** well known for his rock music and his footballing obsession, but less so as a railway modeller.

The layouts in his Beverley Hills mansion, which have featured in three separate issues of *Model Railroader* magazine, include a 1/87 (H0-scale) model of New York's Grand Central Terminal, which the British singer-songwriter built bit by bit over many years while on the road touring. Other serious modellers from the British music scene include Elton John, Jools Holland, Roger Daltrey, John Entwistle, Phil Collins, Eric Clapton and Ringo Starr (no great surprise there, perhaps, given that he narrated two series of *Thomas the Tank Engine*).

▶ **Neil Young:** the Canadian singer/songwriter has a vast Lionel Trains layout and even developed an improved remote control and sound system for the company, which he also serves as a director. Chat show host David Letterman is also a modeller, which resulted in the two of them having a long chat about Lionel Trains live on air when Young was a guest on Letterman's show. Young uses the alter ego Clyde Coil within the model railroading community. (Lionel Trains was the US equivalent of Hornby in Britain and ended up merging with American Flyer, just as Hornby ended up merging with Tri-ang in Britain).

▶ **Tom Hanks:** Hanks is a keen modeller and reportedly jumped at the chance to sign up as a voice actor on the 2004 film *Polar Express*. Other actors said to have been bitten by the bug include David Hasselhoff, Gene Hackman, Donald Sutherland and Mandy Patinkin.

▶ **Frank Sinatra:** at his home in Rancho Mirage, California, Ol' Blue Eyes had an entire 'train cottage' full of Lionel Trains and American Flyer models. His collection was sold with the ranch after his death and was valued at over $1 million.

- ▶ **Walt Disney:** it probably won't surprise you that Walt Disney started with model railroads before progressing to miniature railways he could sit on and drive his friends round his garden on. It's a shame he didn't live long enough to see the Big Thunder Mountain Railroad at his theme parks.

- ▶ **Hermann Göring:** the Luftwaffe commander had two train sets covering 400 square metres in his country home north of Berlin and was often photographed showing them off to visiting dignitaries, including Adolf Hitler. They were typical of the 0-gauge tinplate trains and track made by German toy company Märklin in the 1930s, but Göring had one of the layouts modified with an overhead aeroplane system that allowed him to drop little wooden bombs onto the trains below. This may just have been what convinced Hitler to appoint him Commander-in-Chief of the Luftwaffe in 1935.

- ▶ **Johnny Cash:** a train collector who sang lots of country songs about the American railroad (including 'I've Got a Thing About Trains'), he starred in singing TV commercials for his favourite Lionel Trains in the 1970s.

- ▶ **Tim Berners-Lee:** the English scientist started trainspotting when he attended a London school that sat between two railway tracks. Because he was no good at sport, he also stayed in his room and played with his train set a lot. He made some electronic gadgets to better control his trains, became interested in electronics per se as a direct result of having done so, and went on to invent the World Wide Web. Without train sets, there would be no internet. That's all I'm saying.

TRAINSPOTTING

The decline of trainspotting coincided with the decline of steam from the 1960s onwards, because multiple diesel or electrical units were never going to be as sexy as wooden Pullman carriages rattling through stations behind a screaming steam locomotive, especially if the locomotive in question was 'famous', like *Mallard* or *Flying Scotsman*. But trainspotters do still exist, even if they now find themselves on the endangered species list.

They were always considered a subspecies of the human race by the chattering classes in any event. Even now, the Oxford English Dictionary is somewhat dismissive in its treatment of them, describing a trainspotter as 'a person who collects locomotive numbers as a hobby'. This makes the assumption that the simple trainspotter cannot possibly be interested in the mechanics or look or history of a train, only in its number. Maybe that is indeed true in some cases, but at least the simple souls are out there getting some fresh air.

Perhaps trainspotting might make a comeback in the twenty-first century, though, if high-speed-train advertising takes off in a big way. Known as 'carriage wrapping', examples on Britain's railways have already included a whole East Coast Main Line train covered with the branding of the James Bond film *Skyfall*, and entire Virgin trains promoting *Superman Returns* and *X-Men: Days of Future Past*. If you've got your book handy, the East Coast Main Line InterCity 225 Class 91 locomotive that pulled *Skyfall* was renumbered 91 007 (see what they did there?) for the duration of the advertising campaign. Tick.

BACK TO
THE FUTURE

*Anything is possible on a train: a great meal, a
binge... an intrigue, a great night's sleep...*
FROM PAUL THEROUX'S *THE GREAT RAILWAY BAZAAR* (2008)

As the twenty-first century races ahead, it seems certain that
trains and railways will continue to enjoy something of a revival
around the world. Those who care even a bit for the environment
(it has been estimated that one car consumes half the energy
of an entire high-speed train), or who don't much like sitting
in traffic on increasingly congested roads, or who don't like
airport queues and security checks, can see the obvious benefits
of improved rail travel.

For those who need to get around the cities of the world,
comfortable, efficient urban railways above or below ground
continue to grow. For those who need to get from one city to
another quickly, more high-speed links are proposed, planned or
underway on every continent of the world that isn't covered in
snow and ice. It has even been suggested that maglev trains could
reach 500 miles per hour by the year 2020 – they can get up to
340 miles per hour now.

In continental western Europe and Japan, it remains largely the case that high-speed train beats plane for time, and often also on cost, over distances of up to 500 miles. In Japan, the car is increasingly being dismissed as an expensive, inefficient and environmentally unfriendly plaything when compared to the clean, superfast, efficient bullet trains on offer.

Britain once led the way and gave railways to the world before short-sighted politicians and self-serving businessmen in the second half of the twentieth century undid much of the earlier good work. But we appear to have turned the tide, with significant ongoing investment in high-speed trains, network electrification and, to some extent, biofuels. The Crossrail project has been the largest construction project in Europe for the last ten years and will increase capacity and reduce journey times across London from 2019 onwards. As we have seen, the High Speed 2 (HS2) project will one day offer high-speed services from London to Birmingham, Manchester and Leeds. Britain's railways are already busier than at any time since the 1920s and they are set to get a lot busier still. A National College for High Speed Rail has even been set up in Birmingham to train the next generation of rail infrastructure engineers.

It is perhaps a paradox of our times that we crave the benefits of modern train travel alongside our nostalgia for the golden ages of steam and vintage diesel. Thanks to the efforts of the many volunteers around the world who work tirelessly to preserve the locomotives and railway lines of old, we can have both. But the real thrill will always be the first time we travel on a particular train or line, however old or new it might be, especially when we do so in a different country or travel to a destination that is new to us.

Travelling by train is not just about the journey, but it's not just about the destination either. It's about both, and long may that continue to be so.

SELECT BIBLIOGRAPHY

If this book has inspired you to delve further into the history of rail travel, or to travel more by train, I recommend the following titles to get you moving in the right direction.

Rail historian and broadcaster Christian Wolmar has written several insightful works describing how the railways transformed Britain and beyond, including a general overview called *The Iron Road: The Illustrated History of Railways*. His books on more specific parts of the world or individual topics include *Fire and Steam: How the Railways Transformed Britain*; *Railways and the Raj: How the Age of Steam Transformed India*; *To the Edge of the World: The Story of the Trans-Siberian Railway*; *The Great Railway Revolution: The Epic Story of the American Railroad*; and *Engines of War: How Wars Were Won and Lost on the Railways*.

Julian Holland is another prolific writer on all things railway. His many books include *History of Britain's Railways*, *Great Railway Journeys of the World*, *Exploring Britain's Lost*

Railways and *Voices from the Railways: How the Railways Changed Our Lives.*

The Times travel writer Tom Chesshyre has produced two highly entertaining and informative books on rail travel: *Tales from the Fast Trains: Europe at 186 mph* and *Ticket to Ride: Around the World on 49 Unusual Train Journeys.* The first describes a number of the weekend trips you can take on Eurostar from London, with or without connections to other fast Continental train services when you reach the end of your initial Eurostar journey. The second describes the amazing train journeys he has personally taken around the globe, including within Britain, Continental Europe, India, Sri Lanka, Iran, China, Russia, North Korea and the Australian outback.

Tiny Stations by Dixe Wills is an eccentric look at Britain's 150 railway request stops and the history behind them. It was the inspiration for my own expedition to Corrour in the Scottish Highlands, the highest and remotest railway station in Britain.

Three lavishly illustrated books have been produced to accompany the popular BBC series fronted by Michael Portillo: *Great British Railway Journeys*, *Great Continental Railway Journeys* and *Great American Railroad Journeys.*

Journalist and travel writer Michael Williams slows the pace right down in his books *On the Slow Train* and *On the Slow Train Again*, taking the opportunity to relive a bygone age by taking the slowest train journeys he can find around Britain. He also takes a look at trains and railways past in *The Trains Now Departed.*

Simon Jenkins is the founder of the Railway Heritage Trust. In *Britain's 100 Best Railway Stations*, he encapsulates the history, geography, architecture and social significance of his top 100 stations around Britain.

ACKNOWLEDGEMENTS

My thanks to all at Summersdale for the opportunity and support to write another book on a subject of huge interest to me. On this occasion, I am particularly grateful to Claire Plimmer for the opportunity, Robert Drew for steering the project through to completion with his usual utmost competence and expert editorial skills, and Chris Turton for his helpful comments. My thanks also to Sarah Herman for a meticulous copy-edit, and Roz Andrews for a very helpful proofread, both of which ensured that I stayed very much on track and avoided any unnecessary sidings along the way.

I am also grateful to my good friends Christine and Rowland Hoar and David Howroyd, and to my wife Karen, who together humoured my love of train journeys by accompanying me on my pilgrimage to Corrour, the remotest station in Britain, especially after our first attempt had been foiled by an inconsistency between ScotRail's online booking system and actual timetable. Those fellow members of 'The Famous Five Who Went in Search of Nowhere' were at least rewarded with the magnificence of Rannoch Moor and the relief that a train did turn up in the middle of nowhere to return them to civilisation, unharmed and with far more oxygen in their lungs than they had set out with.

ABOUT THE AUTHOR

Ray Hamilton is a freelance writer and editor, whose lifelong passions are history, languages and travel. He has edited over 90 books on a wide range of subjects, including fiction, politics, history, art, sport, travel, Radio 4 and classical music (in the form of *The Classic FM Quiz Book*). He previously pursued a varied career in government, the highlights of which included multilateral government negotiations in Paris and a number of forays into sub-Saharan Africa. He has written 11 other books, all published by Summersdale:

Military Quotations – Stirring Words of War and Peace (2012)
Le Tour de France – The Greatest Race in Cycling History (2013)
The Joy of Cycling (2013)
The Joy of Golf (2014)
Trains: A Miscellany (2015)
M25: A Circular Tour of the London Orbital (2015)
Knowledge: Stuff You Ought to Know (2016)
A Short History of Britain in Infographics (2017)
For the Love of the Navy (2017)
For the Love of the Army (2017)
Ride: A Fact-Packed Tour through the World of Cycling (2018)

A CELEBRATION OF
THE BRITISH ARMED FORCES

FOR THE LOVE OF THE

ARMY

A COMPANION

RAY HAMILTON

FOR THE LOVE OF THE ARMY

Ray Hamilton

ISBN: 978-1-78685-066-9

Hardback

£9.99

From the heroes, special forces and famous campaigns and battles that make up the British Army's impressive history, through to the remarkable people who serve in her ranks today, this fact-packed book celebrates the achievements and ongoing importance of the UK's land force. Exploring its ground, air support and amphibious capabilities, it also tracks the development of the skills, weaponry and equipment that have been necessary to keep the Army battle-ready and able to face the challenges of the day.

FOREWORD BY
ADMIRAL SIR JONATHON BAND, GCB, DL

FOR THE LOVE OF THE

NAVY

A COMPANION

RAY HAMILTON

FOR THE LOVE OF THE NAVY

Ray Hamilton

ISBN: 978-1-78685-064-5

Hardback

£9.99

Marvel at the magnificent vessels that have always been the backbone of the force; pay homage to the acclaimed naval heroes and the impressive battles that make up its illustrious history; and learn about the remarkable people who serve in the Navy's ranks today as its beating heart, who work to ensure that the Senior Service will retain its reputation for excellence for generations to come.

FOREWORD BY
AIR MARSHAL SIR ROGER AUSTIN KCB AFC

FOR THE LOVE OF THE
AIR FORCE

A COMPANION

NORMAN FERGUSON

FOR THE LOVE OF THE AIR FORCE

Norman Ferguson

ISBN: 978-1-78685-065-2

Hardback

£9.99

With its famous Supermarine Spitfire and the legendary Red Arrows, the RAF has been a pillar of British military operations since its beginnings in 1918. This new miscellany brings together the origins of the RAF, the people who make it tick and the technology that lets it take to the skies, as well as the aviation lingo and time-honoured traditions that characterise the force we know today. Whether you have first-hand RAF experience or you're an enthusiastic supporter from the ground, this remarkable volume will be your guide to the oldest independent air force in the world. Chocks away!

Have you enjoyed this book?
If so, why not write a review on your favourite website?

If you're interested in finding out more about our books, find
us on Facebook at **Summersdale Publishers** and follow us on
Twitter at **@Summersdale**.

Thanks very much for buying this Summersdale book.

www.summersdale.com